CLASSIC
AIRLINERS

76 Older Types, Worldwide, Described and Illustrated in Colour

TOM SINGFIELD

Midland Publishing

This book is dedicated to
the memory of Steve Piercey, whose
enthusiasm for classic 'Propliners' was
an inspiration to many around the world.
He was a great friend and I miss him.

Classic Airliners
© 2000 Tom Singfield

ISBN 1 85780 098 2

First published in 2000 by
Midland Publishing
24 The Hollow, Earl Shilton
Leicester, LE9 7NA, England.
Telephone: 01455 847 256   Fax: 01455 841 805
E-mail: midlandbooks@compuserve.com

Midland Publishing is an imprint of
Ian Allan Publishing Limited

Worldwide distribution (except North America):
Midland Counties Publications
Unit 3 Maizefield, Hinckley Fields,
Hinckley, Leics, LE10 1YF, England.
Telephone: 01455 233 747   Fax: 01455 233 737
E-mail: midlandbooks@compuserve.com

North American trade distribution:
Specialty Press Publishers and Wholesalers
11605 Kost Dam Road, North Branch, MN 55056, USA
Telephone: 651 583 3239   Fax: 651 583 2023
Toll free telephone: 800 895 4585

Design concept and layout
© 2000 Midland Publishing

Printed in China

Photograph on previous page:
Shown prior to delivery in 1959, Northwest Airlines'
first L-188C Electra, N121US, carries the early tail
insignia. (Lockheed Martin Corporation)

Contents

Abbreviations and Glossary

APU	Auxiliary Power Unit – on-board power unit for ancillaries
CofA	Certificate of Airworthiness – national (or international) approval of an aircraft
FAA	Federal Aviation Administration – US legislative and administrative body
FSU	Former Soviet Union – used to denote the regions/nations previously within the USSR
GAZ	Government Aircraft Production Plant – FSU
GE	General Electric – US engine producer
ICAO	International Civil Aviation Organisation – legislative/administrative authority
MTOW	Maximum Take-off Weight
P&W	Pratt & Whitney – US engine producer
P&WC	Pratt & Whitney Canada – subsidiary of P&W
RR	Rolls-Royce – UK engine producer

Arguably the most elegant of all the propliners, the gracious Lockheed Constellation no longer flies commercially. Vern Raburn's California-based 'MATS' L-749 was rescued from storage in Arizona and epitomises the growing interest in the operation of classic airliners. (Lockheed Martin)

Introduction

The current interest in all forms of 'Classic' transport, whether it be aircraft, cars, buses, boats, trains or tractors, has prompted authors and publishers to produce books, magazines and videos to satisfy the enthusiast's desire for a dose of transport nostalgia. With this book, I hope to interest and educate both the dedicated aircraft enthusiast and the casual observer. I am sure both types will enjoy the spread of colour photographs and hopefully some will appreciate the information regarding the 'survivors'.

Some readers like myself can probably recall long-ago days at your local airport when many of the visiting airliners had piston radial engines and the job of 'Airport Security' was to lock the aircraft door at night! Others, myself included, have no memories of the early days of classic airliners when such wondrous machines as Pan Am Stratocruisers and BOAC Britannias graced the tarmac, but despite this, we all enjoy seeing their pictures and reading about them. To the fans of today's modern airliners, people like me who thrill to the sight and sound of a piston engine coughing into life are probably living in the past. But to my mind, today's high technology, high speed, reliable and efficient transports can be pretty uninspiring and nowhere near as interesting as the classic airliners described herein.

With the increase of organised aviation enthusiast tours, I am happy to report that there are now more and more opportunities for enthusiasts to travel the world to seek out classic airliners and photograph and especially fly in them. In addition to the joy rides organised abroad by these tour operators, enthusiasts can now take vintage airliner joy flights at air shows and open days in many countries. It is worth mentioning that in the last couple of years, enthusiasts have been able to try out types such as the Ilyushin IL-14 and 18, Junkers Ju-52, Convair 580, Lisunov Li-2, Lockheed Constellation, Scottish Aviation Twin Pioneer, Vickers Viscount, Antonov An-2 and the Douglas DC-3, 4 and 6.

I would encourage anyone who has an interest in these old aircraft to try to take a ride, particularly in some of the surviving piston-powered airliners. By doing so, you will be able to re-live the 'good' old days of air travel and compare it to today's knee-crushing offerings. They may not appreciate it, but today's harassed passengers jammed into their Airbuses and 777s owe much to the early designers who often struggled with poor materials, inefficient engines, bizarre airline specifications and even government interference to build what we can now consider to be 'Classic Airliners'.

This book follows on from my previous effort, 'Airliners Worldwide', that was published in 1997. Although this book is generally similar in format, in this volume each type featured is generously illustrated with three photographs and the survivors are described in greater detail. Where possible, I have tried to find high-quality colour illustrations that allow readers to see these airliners in different phases of their existence. However, the original goal of an 'early' shot for the heading photo followed by an 'in service' shot and lastly one of a surviving example in its current condition has proved to be a challenge for some types and impossible for others. For instance, colour photographs of BEA or Lufthansa Junkers Ju 52s probably don't exist and the number of high-quality colour images of Aeroflot An-10s and IL-12s in service is probably zero!

The production of this book has prompted some discussion among my colleagues as to the definition of a 'Classic Airliner'. The term 'Classic' tends to get misused these days, but I make no apology for using it to describe the airliners featured. Everyone is entitled to have their own favourite classic airliner types, and although the enclosed are my choices, I'm sure that you will find some airliners within that are indisputably classic and others that qualify for inclusion by age, scarcity or interest. The basic idea behind the book was to include all 'classic' airliner designs that are out of production, have seats for about 15 passengers or more and that have at least one example still in existence somewhere in the world. These parameters have meant that the Scandia can make an appearance (one survivor), but sadly such types as the Languedoc, Marathon, H.P.42, Armagnac, Princess, Tudor, Halton and Flamingo have no place in this book because none have survived. Readers may spot the absence of one or two types that do qualify for this book, but these have had to be excluded due to space restrictions or picture quality. In addition to the 'first generation' jetliners featured,

I have also included such types such as the Boeing 737, 747 and Concorde. These types merit the 'Classic' adjunct because they are all highly significant in the world of air transport.

My own personal Number One Classic has to be the immortal Douglas DC-3. No other aircraft can lay claim to such a distinguished and lengthy career and it is gratifying to know that the DC-3 is more than a museum piece with dozens still earning a living for their owners all over the world. Although all of the current operators realise that they are flying an historic aircraft, many of them are just thankful for the Dakota's enduring qualities of reliability, safety, low maintenance and good economics. They may not pamper their charges with daily polishes and fancy paintwork, they may not even give them the best maintenance, but they fly them to make a profit and I applaud every one of them.

I am delighted that worldwide interest is growing in maintaining classic airliners in airworthy condition. Of course, many old airliners are flown for strictly commercial reasons, but a new breed of owner is appearing who appreciates the significant part in the development of world travel that these often-neglected aircraft achieved. Some of these praiseworthy concerns manage to operate on a purely commercial basis, but you are just as likely to find a restored airliner in the hands of a group of enthusiasts. Airshows used to irritate me because of their bias towards current and vintage military fighters. Thankfully, this is changing, and airshow visitors are often able to see, and perhaps fly in, a selection of beautifully restored classic airliners. Around the world, groups such as the SAA Historic Flight, Lufthansa Traditionsflug, Airliners of America, Air Atlantique, Dutch Dakota Association, Le Caravelle Club, Save a Connie Inc., the Mid Atlantic Air Museum and the Australian Historical Aircraft Restoration Society should all take a bow for their excellent work in saving classic airliners in flying condition for future generations.

The crew of this Braniff International Convair 340, N3429, complete their pre take-off checks while Delta's 440 N4823C waits its turn for departure. (Jay Miller collection)

It is inevitable in a work of this kind that the information published regarding the surviving airliners can soon become out of date and the reported existence of a particular aircraft may be incorrect. I have tried to use the most accurate and up to date sources regarding the survivors as well as using the willing help of many friends and colleagues with access to reliable information. Many of the illustrations within are from my personal collection of colour slides gathered over 25 years and I am afraid that I have not been able to identify every photographer. I apologise to anyone who recognises their uncredited work and thank them whoever they are. A special thanks for help with this book goes to the Gatwick Aviation Society, Ken Ellis, Nick Webb, and Tony Eastwood at the Aviation Hobby Shop.

I would also like to thank the following for help with photographs, advice and information. Colin Ballantine, Erik Bernhard, Tony Best, Peter Bish, Bob Cook, Robert Cote, Bruce Drum, Nigel Eastaway, Bo Edwards (Lockheed Martin), A.Geneve, Mike Green, Jacques Guillem, Scott Henderson, Chris Herbert, Jon Hillier, Peter Hillman, Harry Holmes, Vince Horan, Dave Howell, Kevin Irwin, Tony Merton Jones (Propliner Magazine), Craig Justo (Aero Aspects), Steve Kinder, Bernard King, Fred Knight, Cliff Knox, Josef Krauthäuser, Andy Leaver, Phil Lo Bao, Philippe Loeuillet (Avimage), Chris Mak, Ian Malcolm (African Aviation Slide Service), Peter Marson, The Glen L. Martin Aviation Museum, Matt Martin, Frank McMeiken, Rudolf Merison, Jay Miller, Richard Ness, Robert L North (New England Air Museum), Bob Ogden, Keith Palmer, Simon Pank (Rolls-Royce), Neville Parnell, Alain Peletier, Pierre-Alain Petit, Malcolm Porter, Patrick Vinot Prefontaine, Robert Ruffle, Trevor Scarr (Duxford Aviation Society), Bob Shane, Robbie Shaw, Graham Simons, The Singfield family, Terry Sykes, Julian Temple (Brooklands Museum), Henry Tenby, Frank Tyler, Christian Volpati, Ray Wagner (San Diego Aerospace Museum), Bob Wall, Simon Watson, John Wegg, and Jeff Whitesell.

Please note that the manufacturers' addresses shown in this book are intended to reflect those current when the aircraft concerned were being made; they should not be used for current correspondence.

Tom Singfield,
Horsham, Sussex
March 2000

Above: There's nowhere quite like Sharjah… A daily fee paid to the airport authority allows anyone ramp access to get up close to a variety of classic airliners. Here is your author with a Samara Antonov An-12. (Kevin Irwin)

Below: Thankfully not all old airliners are cut up for scrap at the end of their careers. Here at Duxford the Imperial War Museum/Duxford Aviation Society have on view an impressive and well cared for line up of British types. (Author)

AP	Pakistan	I	Italy	TY	Benin	4R	Sri Lanka
A2	Botswana	JA	Japan	TZ	Mali	4X	Israel
A3	Tonga Islands	JU	Mongolia	T2	Tuvalu	5A	Libya
A40	Oman	JY	Jordan	T3	Kiribati	5B	Cyprus
A5	Bhutan	J2	Djibouti	T7	San Marino	5H	Tanzania
A6	United Arab	J3	Grenada	T9	Bosnia-	5N	Nigeria
	Emirates	J5	Guinea Bissau		Herzogovina	5R	Madagascar
A7	Qatar	J6	St. Lucia	UK	Uzbekistan	5T	Mauretania
A9C	Bahrain	J7	Dominica	UN	Kazakhstan	5U	Niger
B	China, Peoples	J8	St. Vincent and	UR	Ukraine	5V	Togo
	Republic, and		Grenadines	VH	Australia	5W	West-Samoa
	Taiwan	LN	Norway	VN	Vietnam	5X	Uganda
C	Canada	LV	Argentina	VP-A	Anguilla	5Y	Kenya
CC	Chile	LX	Luxembourg	VP-B	Bermuda	6O	Somalia
CN	Morocco	LY	Lithuania	VP-C	Cayman Islands	6V	Senegal
CP	Bolivia	LZ	Bulgaria	VP-F	Falkland Islands	6Y	Jamaica
CS	Portugal	N	USA	VP-G	Gibraltar	7O	Yemen
CU	Cuba	OB	Peru	VP-L	British Virgin	7P	Lesotho
CX	Uruguay	OD	Lebanon		Islands	7Q	Malawi
C2	Nauru	OE	Austria	VP-M	Montserrat	7T	Algeria
C3	Andorra	OH	Finland	VQ-T	Turks and Caicos	8P	Barbados
C5	Gambia	OK	Czech Republic		Islands	8Q	Maldives
C6	Bahamas	OM	Slovak Republic	VT	India	8R	Guyana
C9	Mozambique	OO	Belgium	V2	Antigua and	9A	Croatia
D	Germany	OY	Denmark		Barbuda	9G	Ghana
DQ	Fiji	P	North Korea	V3	Belize	9H	Malta
D2	Angola	PH	Netherlands	V4	St. Kitts and Nevis	9J	Zambia
D4	Cape Verde	PJ	Netherlands		Islands	9K	Kuwait
D6	Comores		Antilles	V5	Namibia	9L	Sierra Leone
EC	Spain	PK	Indonesia	V6	Micronesia	9M	Malaysia
EI	Ireland	PP, PT	Brazil	V7	Marshall Islands	9N	Nepal
EK	Armenia	PZ	Surinam	V8	Brunei	9Q	Dem Rep of Congo
EL	Liberia	P2	Papua New Guinea	XA, XB, XC	Mexico	9U	Burundi
EP	Iran	P4	Aruba	XT	Burkina Faso	9V	Singapore
ER	Moldovia	RA	Russia	XU	Cambodia	9XR	Rwanda
ES	Estonia	RDPL	Laos	XY	Myanmar	9Y	Trinidad and
ET	Ethiopia	RP	Philippines	YA	Afghanistan		Tobago
EW	Belarus	SE	Sweden	YI	Iraq		
EX	Kyrghyztan	SP	Poland	YJ	Vanuatu		
EY	Tadjikistan	ST	Sudan	YK	Syria		
EZ	Turkmenistan	SU	Egypt	YL	Lithuania		
E3	Eritrea	SU-Y	Palestine	YN	Nicaragua		
F	France	SX	Greece	YR	Romania		
F-O	France Overseas	S2	Bangladesh	YS	El Salvador		
G	Great Britain	S5	Slovenia	YU	Serbia-Macedonia		
HA	Hungary	S7	Seychelles	YV	Venezuela		
HB	Switzerland	S9	Sao Tome	Z	Zimbabwe		
	(and Lichtenstein)	TC	Turkey	ZA	Albania		
HC	Ecuador	TF	Iceland	ZK	New Zealand		
HH	Haiti	TG	Guatemala	ZP	Paraguay		
HI	Dominican	TI	Costa Rica	ZS, ZU	South Africa		
	Republic	TJ	Cameroon	Z3	Macedonia		
HK	Colombia	TL	Central African	3A	Monaco		
HL	South Korea		Republic	3B	Mauritius		
HP	Panama	TN	Congo	3C	Equatorial Guinea		
HR	Honduras	TR	Gabon	3D	Swaziland		
HS	Thailand	TS	Tunisia	3X	Guinea		
HZ	Saudi Arabia	TT	Chad	4K	Azerbaijan		
H4	Solomon Islands	TU	Côte d'Ivoire	4L	Georgia		

Originally delivered to Pan American as a Stratocruiser in 1949, Aero Spacelines Boeing 377MG Mini Guppy N1037V 'Spirit of Santa Barbara', is seen at Heathrow in November 1969. The hinges for the swing tail are clearly visible on the starboard rear fuselage. (Author's collection)

AERO SPACELINES GUPPY
Aero Spacelines Inc,
Van Nuys, California,
USA

In the early 1960s, the idea of converting a standard passenger airliner into a large capacity freighter for use by the US space industry was envisaged in the USA by John M Conroy of Van Nuys-based Aero Spacelines Inc. At that time, large rocket sections were transported from the California plants to the test sites in Florida by barge through the Panama Canal. By flying these bulky sections in converted airliners, many days could be saved compared to the long sea journey and the load could also be delivered directly to the launch site.

Conroy bought 27 retired Boeing 377 Stratocruisers (see page 38) and instructed the On Mark Engineering Co to commence conversion of the first 'Pregnant Guppy'. This aircraft, then claimed to be the largest in the world, was created by stretching a Model 377 Stratocruiser by 5.08m (16ft 8in) and replacing the upper 'bubble' of the fuselage with an oversize shell that was built from scratch. Loading was achieved by removing the entire rear fuselage and empennage allowing straight in loading of the cargo from the rear. The Pregnant Guppy first flew in September 1962 and from June 1963 it was employed carrying Saturn rocket sections in the USA.

The first 'Super Guppy', with an even larger capacity fuselage and turboprop engines, flew on 31st August 1965 at Van Nuys. This aircraft was converted from the unique P&W

T-34 turboprop-powered YC-97J. Because of the huge fuselage and extra power, the Super Guppy was built with an extended tail fin to provide better control. Loading was much quicker on this design because the entire nose section was on hinges allowing entry for the cargo from the front. Four further examples of the Super Guppy 201 were then completed, two in the USA and two by UTA at Le Bourget. These four were flown on behalf of Airbus Industrie transporting bulky fuselages and wings between the Airbus Industrie factories at Bremen, Finkenwerder, Manchester, Naples, St. Nazaire and Toulouse. They have now been retired and their job has been taken over by the equally impressive A300-600ST Super Transporter, the 'Beluga'.

A single 377MG Mini Guppy was built that retained the Stratocruiser's R-4360 Double Wasp radial engines and flying surfaces. This had a hinged 'swingtail' for loading and first flew in May 1967.

Next to be built was a single Mini Guppy 101 with a fuselage similar in size to the Mini Guppy, but with Allison 501-D22C turboprop engines. This first flew in March 1970 but crashed on a test flight two months later before entering service. Studies for further Guppies included one with six Allison engines and the 'Colossal Guppy', based on a converted B-52 bomber with a 40ft diameter fuselage!

Of the eight conversions completed, six survive including one still in service. The unique T-34 powered Super Guppy is preserved in its NASA livery at the Pima Air Museum in Arizona. The Mini Guppy is preserved at the Tillamook Naval Air Station Museum in Oregon and three Super Guppy 201s are preserved at Bruntingthorpe, Finkenwerder and Toulouse. NASA bought the remaining ex-Airbus Super Guppy 201 and it is currently flying from Los Alamitos Army Airfield in California in support of the International Space Station programme.

Specifications (for the Guppy 201)

Span: 47.62m (156ft 3in)
Length: 43.84m (143ft 10in)
Engines: Four 3,666kW (4,912 ehp)
    Allison 501-D22C turboprops
Cruise speed: 407km/h (220kts)
Payload: 24,494kg (54,000lb)
Volume: 1,100 cu.m (38,846 cu.ft)

Re-registered N422AU in 1981, the Boeing 377MG Mini Guppy was bought by Erikson Air-Crane of Central Point, Oregon. In 1995 this aircraft was flown to the Tillamook NASM for preservation. (Bob Shane)

The future looks bright for this preserved Super Guppy 201 F-BPPA. Photographed at Toulouse in February 1999, it is preserved by Ailes Anciennes Toulouse who also have a collection of airliners including a Caravelle, DC-3 and a Breguet Deux Ponts. (Bob Wall)

Photographed at Le Bourget in June 1979 is the first French-built Concorde F-WTSS. This aircraft first flew in March 1969, one month before the British-built G-BSST, and was retired to the Musée de l'Air in 1973. (Jacques Guillem)

AEROSPATIALE/BAC CONCORDE

British Aircraft Corporation Ltd, Filton, England and Sud-Aviation, Toulouse, France

In November 1962, the governments of France and Great Britain signed an agreement initiating collaboration on the design and construction of a Supersonic Transport (SST) airliner. Prior to this, both countries had carried out design work on their own versions of an SST, France with the delta winged 'Super Caravelle', and Britain with the BAC 223. However both countries decided that although it was feasible to build an SST, the costs involved were beyond any individual company.

After much deliberation, the name 'Concorde' was chosen, and the design emerged as an elegant slim fuselage with a pointed nose, together with a highly complex ogival delta wing. The technical complexities in producing an SST threw up many problems, each of which were expensive and time con-suming to solve. Much discussion concerned the Concorde's maximum speed. Protection of the airframe from high temperatures caused by air friction while cruising between Mach 2.5 and 3.0 would have involved the considerable use of expensive heat-resistant metals, so a compromise was made where the cruising speed was restricted to Mach 2.2. This decision allowed designers to limit the use of expensive titanium and stainless steel in the Concorde. Another problem involved crew visibility at low speeds. Here, the solution was the 'droop snoot' nose that is lowered for landing and take-off. Just as complicated are the engine nacelles. They are

fitted with a multitude of inlet and exhaust devices to enable the engines to operate effectively at subsonic and supersonic speeds.

Most prospective buyers specified trans-Atlantic range in order to attract the lucrative business market. The manufacturer's promised performance brought 'commitments' for a total of 80 Concordes from several of the worlds' major airlines, including Pan Am, Lufthansa and Qantas.

Design consultations delayed the start of prototype construction until February 1965. Two were built, one at Toulouse and the other at Filton and the French-built prototype was the first to fly on 2nd March 1969. A long development programme further delayed Concorde's entry into revenue service until 1976, by which time only British Airways and Air France remained as customers. The lack of any other orders and the staggering costs involved in creating this technological marvel caused an enormous financial loss for the two country's manufacturers and taxpayers.

For many years, the anti-noise lobby tried to get Concorde banned because of its sonic boom and its ear-splitting engine noise at take-off. Because of its noise, the Concorde is severely restricted to where it can land and is banned from supersonic flight over much of the world's landmass. Despite this, Concorde has now been in regular, and profitable, supersonic airline service for over 20 years without a serious accident. In the last few

years British Airways have spent millions of pounds refitting their Concorde fleet, ensuring that this unique airliner can remain safe and reliable into the 21st century.

In May 1999, Air France announced they had carried their one millionth Concorde passenger on the New York to Paris service, and that despite a reappearance of a movement to remove Concorde from the USA due to its noise, they vowed to continue their daily supersonic schedule.

Apart from the Concordes on scheduled services seen in Paris, London and New York, many other airports have allowed individual visits for special flights and airshows. After 30 years of flying, Concorde still causes controversy but it continues to turn the head of any spectator, either away from the noise or towards it to appreciate a true piece of aviation history. From the 20 Concordes built, 13 are in service, one has been scrapped, two are stored at Filton and Toulouse and preserved Concordes are on display at Duxford, Yeovilton, Orly, and Le Bourget.

Specifications

Span: 25.56m (83ft 10in)
Length: 62.10m (203ft 9in)
Engines: Four 170.2kN (38,050lb)
  Rolls-Royce/ SNECMA Olympus 593 Mk.610
  turbojets with afterburners
Cruise speed: 2,179km/h (1,176kts)
Accommodation: 144 maximum

Taxying out from Heathrow's Terminal 4 for a service to New York is Concorde 102 G-BOAC. The incredibly complex wing design and the improved forward visibility from the drooped nose are evident in this photo. (Author)

This remarkable Concorde colour scheme was only carried for about ten days. Air France Concorde 101 F-BTSD appeared in the new Pepsi colours for an advertising campaign at Gatwick in April 1996. (Robbie Shaw)

Ambassador Mk.II G-AMAE was bought by Dan-Air London from Australian airline Butler Air Transport. Its last service was with Dan-Air on 30th September 1970 after which it was flown to Lasham where it was scrapped in December 1971. (Graham Simons collection)

AIRSPEED AS.57 AMBASSADOR

Airspeed Ltd
Christchurch Aerodrome
Hampshire, England

At the height of the Second World War, the Brabazon committee recommended several civil airliner projects to the British government for post war commercial use. Among their recommendations, the Type IIA was proposed as a Douglas DC-3/Dakota replacement for European short-haul services. The tough challenge of bettering the faithful 'Dak' was accepted by the small Airspeed company based at the former Government shadow factory at Christchurch Aerodrome.

During their design work, Airspeed correctly predicted that future commercial transport in Europe would require a bigger, faster and more comfortable airliner. Their design for the Ambassador therefore grew and evolved into an all-metal, tricycle undercarriage airliner with two powerful piston radial engines mated to a high aspect ratio, high-mounted wing and a sleek pressurised fuselage. To achieve high speeds, great attention was applied to the aerodynamics. This included the design of the low-drag cowlings on the 'quick change' power cells that were able to open up like flower petals allowing superb access to the engines. Airspeed also proposed other variants based on the Ambassador including a dedicated freighter, the 'Ayrshire' military transport and an armed maritime reconnaissance aircraft. All these projects were cancelled as was the Ambassador Mk.II powered by four turboprops.

The first of the three prototypes was flown by the famous test pilot G B S Errington from Christchurch on 10th July 1947. After a great deal of discussions, and despite BEA's interest in the promising Vickers Viscount, they grudgingly made a £3 million order for 20 Ambassadors in September 1948. Sadly, after de Havilland bought Airspeed in 1948, sales prospects for the Ambassador disappeared and only BEA's order was completed. The type was known as the 'Elizabethan' with BEA, whose first scheduled Ambassador service was to Paris in March 1952.

BEA's 'Elizabethan' services were gradually replaced by the Vickers Viscount from 1956, and after retirement from BEA service in 1957/58, three aircraft were sold to Butler Air Transport in Australia, while others found their way to Autair, BKS, Dan-Air Services and Globe Air. The Royal Jordanian Air Force and Shell Aviation each acquired two Ambassadors for executive duties and the prototype aircraft later found valuable use as a flying engine test bed for Bristols, Napier and Rolls-Royce.

Probably the last Ambassador to fly was the one operated by the Decca Navigator Company as an airborne laboratory from 1963 until it was retired in 1971. This aircraft was often used as a company 'shuttle' for the Paris Air Show. Sadly, it was scrapped while in fine condition at West Malling in the early 1970s.

Very few Airspeed designed aircraft of any type have managed to survive. You may find an Oxford, a Horsa or a Consul preserved in a museum here and there, but I doubt whether you could find an Envoy, a Ferry or a Courier anywhere. Thanks however to the staff of the much loved, but departed British airline Dan-Air, a single example of Airspeed's final and most elegant commercial aircraft, the Ambassador, is safely preserved among the classic airliners at the Imperial War Museum, Duxford.

This aircraft, G-ALZO, completed Dan-Air's last official 'Lizzy' service, a return trip Gatwick-Jersey on 26th September 1971; it was then flown to Dan-Air's maintenance base at Lasham Airfield in Hampshire for preservation alongside their Avro York. Both of these aircraft were later moved to Duxford where they are undergoing full restoration as static exhibits in Dan-Air London colours.

Specifications

Span: 35.05m (115ft 0in)
Length: 24.99m (82ft 0in)
Engines: Two 1939kW (2600hp)
  Bristol Centaurus 661 piston radials
Cruise speed: 386 km/h (240mph)
Accommodation: 47-60

The tiny viewing deck at Jersey Airport is now sadly closed. Great views such as this shot of BKS's Ambassador 2 G-ALZT taxying out in August 1966 will never be repeated. (Harry Holmes)

The world's only survivor from the 23 Ambassadors built is seen here part way through a lengthy restoration with the Duxford Aviation Society in August 1999. It will be at least two years before G-ALZO reappears in full Dan-Air London colours. (Author)

In March 1992, the forbidding and freezing cold ramp at Ulan Bataar in Outer Mongolia was host to more than 30 Mongolian Airlines An-2s in a variety of colour schemes. Since then, many of them have been scrapped. (Colin Ballantine)

ANTONOV An-2 & SAMC YUNSHUJI Y-5

Antonov Design Bureau, 1 Tupolev Prospect, Kiev 252062, Ukraine
PZL Mielec, Wojska Polskiego 3, PL-39-300 Mielec, Poland
Shijiazhuang Aircraft Mfg Corp, PO Box 164, Shijiazhuang, Hebei 050062, China

With a total production figure in the region of 20,000, the An-2 (NATO reporting name 'Colt') is the world's best selling commercial aircraft.

After the Second World War, Oleg Antonov's design bureau set out to produce an aircraft that would meet a specification proposed by the USSR Ministry of Agriculture and Forestry for a multi-task machine. The resulting An-2 that first flew on 31st August 1947 was, and still is, a remarkable aeroplane, strong, simple, reliable, adaptable and long-lived. The fact that uncompleted 'new' An-2s were still available from PZL in Poland fifty years after the first flight, is nothing short of incredible.

After 1960, the PZL works at Mielec, in Poland, took over full production responsibility except for the An-2M which continued to be built in Russia. Since the first Polish-built An-2 flew on 23rd October 1961, PZL-Mielec has made continuous improvements to the airframe allowing the current versions an in-service life of 15,900 hours. More than 90% of the 10,000 Polish-built An-2s were exported, most of them to the USSR.

Thanks to its huge wing area and high-lift devices, the An-2 is remarkably docile in the air. It has a stalling speed of 95 km/h (52kts) combined with a STOL performance allowing a grass take-off run of only 170m. Many different versions were built including the An-2T (transport – 1500kg freight or 12

passengers), An-2P (12 passengers), An-2TP (cargo/passenger), An-2V Floatplane, An-2S Ambulance (6 stretchers plus attendants), An-2PK (5-seat executive), An-2L Water Bomber, An-2Skh/An-2M agricultural models and the Polish-built Utility An-2R (1300kg duster/sprayer). The home-produced An-2M can be identified its larger, square-shaped tail fin. A turboprop-powered An-3 was also developed and is currently available as a conversion for existing An-2s.

The first Chinese-built Antonov An-2 (known as the Yun-5) was completed at Nanchang as the 'Fongshu 2' in December 1957. The current Y-5B agriculture and forestry model, with a Chinese-built HS5 engine and avionics, first flew in 1989. Other Chinese variants include the utility Y-5N and the passenger Y-5C.

Since the collapse of the Soviet Union, many An-2s that were formerly flown by the various Aeroflot divisions are now operated by the newly formed airlines such as Air Ukraine and Tyumenaviatrans. The type is still common in the FSU and, despite various replacement designs; hundreds of An-2s will most certainly still be in service for the foreseeable future.

In order to raise valuable foreign currency, many FSU operators have tried to sell their redundant An-2s to the West. Several examples have been sold 'abroad' and found new lives in the Western world giving scenic

flights, carrying parachutists or as 'toys' for imaginative and enthusiastic pilots. The most incredible use of an An-2 is probably by the company in Russia that uses their An-2s as aerial platforms for ballet dancing at 8000ft! The Moscow Flying Ballet commenced performances in October 1995 with ballerinas who perform various routines on the roof of the flying Antonov while wearing tutus and goggles! Amazingly they refuse to wear parachutes because they say they restrict their movements! Rather cruelly, the ballerinas have nicknamed their historic steed 'The Flying Cow'.

Specifications (for the PZL built An-2P)

Span: 18.18m (59ft 8in)
Length: 12.74m (41ft 9in)
Engine: One 746kw (1,000hp) PZL Kalisz ASz-62IR radial piston engine
Cruise speed: 185km/h (100kts)
Accommodation: Maximum 19, normally 12

This Polish-built Antonov An-2TP was delivered to the East German airline Interflug in August 1968. Based at Berlin Schönefeld airport, it was sold in 1990 to Berliner Special Flug. Note the modified cockpit and cabin windows. (Author's collection)

This late model An-2TP was built in Poland around 1990 and registered in Czechoslovakia. In 1994 it was placed on the new Slovakian register as OM-UIN and is seen here at White Waltham in September where I was fortunate to have a flight in it. (Author)

The elusive Antonov An-8 was rarely seen by westerners until organised tours for aircraft enthusiasts were made into the Soviet Union in the 1980s. Here is CCCP-13323 at Myachkovo in September 1991; it crashed in December 1993. (Author's collection)

ANTONOV An-8

Antonov Design Bureau
1 Tupolev Prospect, 252062 Kiev
Ukraine

Back in the days of the 'cold war' of the early 1950s, the Soviet Union was not concerned if their latest aeronautical development was unknown in the West. Indeed, with a guaranteed home market for any new airliner and the occasional prospect of export sales to friendly countries, they were hardly likely to advertise their new products in the pages of 'Flight International'.

It was in these circumstances that the groundbreaking twin-engined An-8 was born. Hardly noticed by the Western aviation press, the An-8 was however a significant milestone in the design progress of Antonov transports that eventually led via the An-10 (see page 18), to the remarkable four-engine An-12 (see page 20) which formed the backbone of the Soviet transport fleet for many years.

Until recent use in the UAE, South Africa and Sri Lanka, the An-8 (NATO reporting name 'Camp') was virtually unknown outside the USSR. Designed around 1952/53, it first flew in 1955 powered by two Kuznetsov NK-6 turboprops and made its first public appearance at the Tushino Air Show in 1956. Up to 200 were built at the Antonov factory at GAZ No. 34 in Tashkent. The type first entered service with the Soviet armed forces as a military transport in 1956 and it was sometimes seen with Aeroflot titles, but this was a common practice with Soviet military transport aircraft and did not signify genuine ownership by Aeroflot. Around 1979, the

small fleet of military An-8s were withdrawn from front-line service and several were transferred to Aeroflot as freighters.

Even though it was only built in relatively small numbers, the An-8 was considered to be a remarkable aircraft. Antonov had no experience building highly stressed all-metal aircraft of this size, so the resulting high quality design was all the more surprising. Most significant of the advanced features provided was the high wing layout with a full-width rear loading ramp, which, combined with the high tailplane, enabled direct loading of freight into the unpressurised 2.5m square rear fuselage. The high wing which kept the propellers well clear of the ground and the strong, retractable, twin-tandem main undercarriage housed in neat fuselage fairings assisted operations from unprepared fields. Military An-8s had a rear gun turret at the base of the fin, but this is now faired over for 'civilian' use.

The An-8 was given the nickname 'Kit' (Whale) by its crews. This caused one Moscow company to adopt the name 'Kosmos i Transport Aviakompania', allowing them to paint KIT titles on their An-8s and even have a cartoon of a whale on the tail.

A few dozen are reported as stored or preserved in the FSU, while only a handful survive in airworthy condition. In the late 1990s, flyable examples of this very rare aircraft could be found on freight services in

the darkest corners of Africa, in Sri Lanka and at Sharjah in the UAE. Judging by the condition of an An-8 I inspected at Sharjah, some of them lead a tough life. They are obviously flown into unmade strips that throw up dirt and stones on to the elevators and it is doubtful if they receive more than basic maintenance. In March 1999, a new country to operate the type was noted when Singapore-based Air Mark added an An-8 to their fleet.

Specifications

Span: 37.00m (121ft 4in)
Length: 30.74m (100ft 10in)
Engines: Two 3,863ekW (4,190ehp)
Progress AI-20D turboprops
Cruise speed: 480km/h (255kts)
Accommodation: 48
Payload: 16,750kg (36,900lb)

Orenburg Central airport had four An-8s when visited by the Alpha Mike Tour in April 1997. Photographed here are two aircraft recently retired by Kit Space and Transport complete with whale emblems on the tail. The Russian nickname for the An-8 is Kit (whale). (Mike Green)

Until fairly recently, the Soviet propliner haven at Sharjah in the UAE was home to half a dozen An-8s. Most of them have now gone, but this Sri Lankan-registered example was seen there in February 1999. Seven months later this aircraft was on relief work in East Timor. (Avimage)

Amongst the amazing collection of Soviet-built airliners at the Monino Museum is this rare Antonov An-10 CCCP-11213. Aeroflot An-10 services were stopped in 1973 and most survivors were scrapped. (Author's collection)

ANTONOV An-10

Antonov Design Bureau
1 Tupolev Prospect, 252062 Kiev
Ukraine

Design work on the Antonov An-10 (NATO reporting name Cat) began in late 1955. Basically, it was an upgraded, enlarged and pressurised version of the An-8 (see page 16) designed specifically for the airline market in the USSR. The aircraft was developed alongside a freighter version with a modified rear fuselage and tail unit which evolved into the Antonov An-12 (see page 20).

Like the An-12, the An-10 was fitted with AI-20 turboprops; however the two prototypes had Kuznetsov NK-4s which in trials, showed poor fuel consumption. The An-10 first flew at Kiev on 7th March 1957 but the type had to endure the usual series of test flying and non-passenger services before it was placed in Aeroflot passenger service on the Moscow to Simferopol route on 22nd July 1959. During these tests, the An-10, now named 'Ukraina' had shown severe directional stability problems. These problems were rectified after the aircraft had been drastically re-engineered with anhedral on the outer wings and by the fitting of various aerodynamic devices to the rear fuselage and tailplane.

When the prototype was shown to the press at Vnukovo in July 1957, the 84-seat main cabin areas revealed nothing unusual; however the rear cabin was fitted out as a children's play area. Great idea, providing you are not trying to grab some sleep in the next row!

In December 1959 an example of the revised An-10A flew to Washington in the USA and on the 10th of February 1960, one entered service from Moscow and Leningrad. In August 1960, an An-10A made history by inaugurating Aeroflot's 'Great Circle' route from Moscow to Khabarovsk via Syktyvkar, Noril'sk and Yakutsk. The 'A' version had been announced in 1958, and had a 2m (6ft 7in) fuselage stretch that allowed for an additional 2 rows of seats giving a standard load of 100 passengers, but with the potential of seating over 120 in a high density, six-abreast layout. Early versions of the An-10A were fitted with large 'end-plates' on the tail plane, but these were replaced by twin ventral fins in the definitive version. By 1963 the An-10A was flying the important daily Aeroflot service between Kiev (Borispol) and Sochi (Adler).

Despite gaining several records and a Russian claim that it was the most economic airliner in the world, the An-10/10A was not successful. By the time it was withdrawn from civil operations in August 1973, at least 42 of the approximately 100 built had crashed. The final straw for the An-10A was a tragic accident near Kharkov on the 18th May 1972 when all 108 passengers and crew were killed.

No An-10/10A sales were made outside the USSR, and very few enthusiasts have ever seen one. At least three are currently preserved at Monino, Baranovochi, and Samara, while a similar number are to be found 'dumped' at various airfields in the FSU. The easiest 'Ukraina' to see is the Aeroflot An-10A preserved in the fantastic Air Force Museum at Monino, east of Moscow.

Specifications (for the An-10A)

Span: 38.00m (124ft 8¼in)
Length: 34.00m (111ft 6in)
Engines: Four 2,983 kW (4015 ehp) Ivchenko AI-20 turboprops
Cruise speed: 630 km/h (391mph)
Accommodation: Maximum 126, normally 100

In August 1993, a group of enthusiasts discovered the mortal remains of An-10 CCCP-11171 at the Riga-Spilve airport in Latvia. The smart blue Aeroflot livery has faded to nothing in the 20 years of storage. (Kevin Irwin)

Many Soviet-built airliners have found new careers after their retirement from airline service. This An-10 (CCCP-11200) inscribed 'Antoshka' was reportedly used as a cinema and theatre at Samara in May 1993. (Mike Green)

This very smart Voronezh-built Aeroflot An-12B CCCP-11361 displays the early red colour scheme during a freight charter at Heathrow in September 1966. Note that the rear gun turret has been covered over. (Author's collection)

ANTONOV An-12

Antonov Design Bureau
1 Tupolev Prospect, 252062 Kiev
Ukraine

Even if the new Antonov An-70 propfan freighter is eventually produced in large numbers, it is certain that the trusted and reliable An-12 will continue to provide excellent service for both civil and military operators well into the 21st century.

The An-12 design was developed from the 90-seater An-10 'Ukraina' passenger airliner (see page 18), and was produced specifically to meet a Soviet Air Force requirement for a turboprop freighter. Compared to the An-10, the An-12 had a completely new rear fuselage with a rear loading ramp and a tail gunner position at the base of the fin. The prototype, powered by four Kuznetsov NK-4 turboprops, first flew in December 1957, and large-scale production at Tashkent, Voronezh and Irkutsk continued until 1972. As a confirmation of the An-12's excellence, its designers were presented with the Lenin Prize in 1962. Antonov also developed a mixed passenger/freight version with a small, pressurised passenger cabin seating 14 situated behind the cockpit.

The An-12 (NATO reporting name 'Cub') became the Soviet's equivalent of the Lockheed C-130 Hercules and was sold to most of the air forces and many airlines of the countries that had allegiances with the Soviet Union. Like the Hercules, the An-12's large rear cargo ramp permitted direct loading from the back of a truck and also the delivery of cargo in flight by using extraction parachutes.

A rail-mounted 2.5-ton overhead gantry crane assists in the loading of bulky cargo and the typically robust undercarriage allows the An-12 to operate from grass, sand, pebbles or snow. The type has also been seen with a ski undercarriage on Polar services. Apart from the usual freight/troop transportation, the An-12 was built for a variety of specific tasks and around 30 different variants were produced. For civil operations, the rear tail gun turret is often removed and the area faired over.

In a similar deal to the An-24/Yunshuji Y-7, licence production of the An-12 commenced in 1969 at the Shaanxi Aircraft Co factory in Yanliang, China. The Yunshuji Y-8 was an upgraded version of the An-12BK with four 3,170kW (4,250shp) Zhuzhou WJ6 engines. The Chinese-built version can be differentiated from the Antonov by its longer, more pointed nose. The Y-8 first flew in 1974 and more than 50 have been completed, mostly for military use. Production of the Y-8 reportedly stopped in 1993. Several versions are available including the Y-8B, the fully pressurised Y-8C, and the Y-8D with Western avionics.

Over 150 civilian An-12s are believed to be in operation currently. Most are to be found in the FSU, but the Soviet-built propliner havens at Sharjah and Fujairah in the UAE always have a few on the ramp while Afghanistan, Angola, Bulgaria, Lesotho, Sri Lanka and the Sudan have all had small fleets recently. In recent

times the freight ramp at Kent International (Manston) in the UK has been the home of a couple of An-12s that fly ad hoc freight services to Europe and North Africa.

Several military examples are preserved in the FSU and the Indian Air Force have kept one for their Air Force Museum in Delhi. At least two Aeroflot An-12s are preserved at Aktyubinsk and Magadan and many more are in use as instructional airframes or workmen's huts.

Specifications

Span: 38.00m (124ft 8in)
Length: 33.10m (108ft 7in) An-12BP 34.05m (111ft 8in)
Engines: Four 2,493kW (3,495shp) Ivchenko AI-20K or M turboprops
Cruise speed: 670kmh (361kts)
Accommodation: 14 passengers
Payload: 20,000kg (44,090lb)

In need of a good wash to remove the smoke deposits from its Ivchenko turboprops is Balkan's LZ-BAE. It was photographed taxying out from the Zurich freight ramp before departure to Sofia in March 1991. (Author)

The extended nose of the Chinese-built Yunshuji Y-8 is evident in this photo of Y-8C number 182. It displays the markings of AVIC, the Aviation Industries of China. (Author's collection)

This immaculate An-22 was photographed at Le Bourget in May 1981 in connection with the Paris Air Show. A production version, CCCP-09336 was built at Tashkent in 1971. (Christian Volpati)

ANTONOV An-22

Antonov Design Bureau
1 Tupolev Prospect, 252062 Kiev
Ukraine

Design of this, the world's largest turboprop aircraft, began in the Ukraine around 1962 with the intention of producing a long range, large capacity strategic transport for the Soviet military forces.

The construction of three pre-production aircraft at Kiev-Svyetoshino entailed the manufacture of massive fuselage forgings and the stamping of components with a unique 75,000-ton press. When the prototype An-22 first flew on 27th February 1965, it was the largest aircraft in the world. Four months later, it made its debut appearance in the West at the 1965 Paris Air Show. In later years An-22s made many visits to the show delivering and collecting the entire Soviet aeronautical and space industry's display pavilion.

Design features of the An-22 (NATO reporting name 'Cock') include a rear-loading ramp, two roof-mounted 10-ton gantry cranes running on rails, a reinforced titanium cargo floor and a crew rest/passenger compartment behind the cockpit with seating for 29. The cavernous 4.4m x 4.4m (14ft 5in x 14ft 5in) and 33.0m (108' 3") long cabin was provided with Antonov's typical rear loading ramp that allowed self-driven military items such as the T-62, T-72 and T-80 battle tanks to be driven in directly. A less aggressive use for the An-22 was the transportation of outsize civilian loads, especially those which could not be carried by rail. These included riverboats, civil engineering equipment, bridge trusses and

buses. One An-22 was modified with a third central tail fin and various attachment points to allow the transportation of new wings for the An-124 on its roof!

Named after the giant son of Poseidon, Greek God of the Ocean, the An-22 'Antei' (in English - Antheus) was designed, like many Soviet aircraft, for operation away from normal runway surfaces. Its 12-wheel main undercarriage, complete with in-flight adjustable tyre pressures, allowed operation from snow, grass or dirt. On a series of trips to the Samotlor oil field, An-22s delivered an entire gas turbine generator for a power station onto a snow runway 1,200m long.

The An-22 holds many payload-to-height and speed records. In 1967, a crew headed by the Hero of the Soviet Union, I E Davydov, flew a prepared cargo consisting of metal blocks weighing 100.4 tons (220,500lb) to an altitude of 7,848m (25,748ft). In 1972, the famous Russian woman pilot Marina Popovich set ten speed records including one of over 600km/h on a 1,000km flight.

The type was also used to export new military hardware and aircraft to foreign buyers. Although these flights abroad were under military control, overflight and landing permission for them was made easier by the use of Aeroflot callsigns. Only one An-22 appeared in full military camouflage and markings, the rest carried the standard Aeroflot blue cheat-line and titles.

After the three pre-production aircraft were completed, the main production line was moved to GAZ.34 in Tashkent where a further 65 An-22s were built. From 1973 until production finished in 1975, Factory No.34 switched to an upgraded An-22A version. This had revised navigation equipment and electrics and an APU mounted in the starboard main gear housing.

Current use is extremely limited, the type having been ousted by the pure jet An-124 and Ilyushin IL-76 freighters. Many of the surviving examples appear to be grounded at Ivanovo and at Tver/Kalinin, 160km northwest of Moscow.

Specifications

Span: 64.40m (211ft 4in)
Length: 57.80m (189ft 7in)
Engines: Four 11,186kW (15,000shp)
  Kuznetsov NK-12MA turboprops
Cruise speed: 640 km/h (400mph)
Payload: 80,000kg (176,350lb)

This 1995 shot of Ukrainian registered An-22 UR-09307 shows the position of the crew-entry door in the portside wheel housing. The Antonov Design Bureau operates this aircraft on worldwide freight charters. (Author's collection)

RA-08836 is believed to be the last An-22 built. First flown in December 1975, it was photographed in February 1993 at Mirow with the CCCP prefix changed to RA and a Russian Federation flag on the tail. (Author's collection)

A long way from home in June 1972 was Lina Congo's An-24PB TN-ABY at Le Bourget. Built in Kiev in 1971, it was later transferred to the Congo Air Force and may still exist at Brazzaville. (Author's collection)

ANTONOV An-24

Antonov Design Bureau
1 Tupolev Prospect, 252062 Kiev
Ukraine

Designed to replace the Lisunov Li-2 and Ilyushin IL-14 (see page 106) in Aeroflot service, the turboprop An-24 was a great success and was sold all around the world. Using a high wing and a strong twin-wheeled undercarriage, it fulfilled the usual Aeroflot requirements for easy loading and the ability to operate from small airfields with unprepared runways. The high wings also helped to keep the propellers clear of debris thrown up during landing and take off. When it first entered service with Aeroflot, the Western press took little notice of the neat 44-seater with engines specially designed for it, but its rugged and practical design evolved and it became the forerunner of the An-26, the An-30, the An-32 and the Chinese built Y-7.

Design work on the An-24 (NATO reporting name 'Coke') commenced in 1958 and the prototype was first flown from Kiev in December 1959. After completing its flying trials, including early freight services with Aeroflot, the An-24 commenced regular passenger services in October 1962. Production lines were set up at Kiev-Svyyetoshino, Ulan Ude and Irkutsk, and the type became a financial success for the Soviets being exported to 23 countries. Foreign customers included Air Guinée, Air Mali, Balkan Bulgarian, Cubana, CAAC, Egyptair, Iraqi Airways, Interflug, Mongolian Airlines, LOT and Tarom. The type was also operated by the Air Forces of the Soviet Union

and other countries as a freighter/troop transport.

Several versions were built including the standard 50-seat An-24B (An-24V in Cyrillic letters), the multi-role An-24B Series II with water injection engines, and the An-24TV and RT freighters. The An-24RV and the RT have a 900kg (1,985lb) thrust Tumansky Ru-19A-300 auxiliary turbojet in the starboard engine nacelle for use as an APU and to provide extra performance in hot-and-high conditions. An An-24P (Protivopozharny) was also built to carry fire-fighting parachutists and equipment.

Approximately 42 Soviet-built An-24s were bought by the Chinese State airline CAAC commencing in 1969. The Chinese obviously thought that the type was ideal for their domestic services because they swiftly organised permission from the Soviets to allow the production of the An-24 in China under licence. The Xian Aircraft Company built the Y-7 (Yunshuji 7/Transport Aircraft No.7) with Chinese-built Dongan 5A-1 engines and a slightly wider fuselage and longer wings. The first flight of a production-model Y-7 was in 1984. A further upgrade of the Y-7 is the Y-7-100 with new avionics and interior while the Y-7-100A, converted from a Y-7 in Hong Kong, has distinctive winglets. Dozens of the Y-7 series are still in regular use in China where China Northern Airlines has the largest fleet.

Although production stopped in 1979, the An-24 is still widely used inside the FSU.

Several hundred still provide reliable passenger and freight services and Air Kazakhstan, Air Ukraine and Dalavia in Khabarovsk operate large fleets. Outside of the FSU small numbers of serviceable An-24s soldier on in Africa, China, Cuba, Korea and Mongolia. Very few civil An-24s are preserved; one Cubana aircraft is in the Lenin Park, Havana and the FSU museums at Monino and Ulyanovsk both have examples.

Specifications

Span: 29.20m (95ft 9in)
Length: 23.53m (77ft 2in)
Engines: Two 1,901ekW (2,550ehp) or 2,103ekW (2,820ehp) Progress AI-24 (Series 2) or AI-24T turboprops
Cruise speed: 450kmh (243kts)
Accommodation: 50 maximum

Rarely photographed were the seven Interflug An-24Bs. DM-SBF was captured on film at Berlin in October 1974, two years before it was sold to Hang Khong Vietnam Airlines. (Jean-Marie Magendie)

Despite the hundreds of An-24s built, the type is becoming rare outside the FSU. I was lucky to shoot this Air Moldova An-24RV ER-47698 from the roof of the famous Emmantina hotel in Athens in March 1999. (Author)

After many months of searching for a BEA 'Red square' Argosy photograph, I am grateful to Christian Volpati for allowing me to use his lovely shot of BEA Argosy 222 G-ASXN at Paris Le Bourget in August 1968. (Christian Volpati)

ARMSTRONG WHITWORTH AW.650 ARGOSY

Sir W G Armstrong Whitworth Aircraft Ltd, Baginton Aerodrome, Coventry and Bitteswell Aerodrome Leicestershire. (Later Hawker Siddeley Aviation)

The AW.650 Argosy, medium range, twin boom freighter evolved from designs for a general-purpose transport that were initiated in 1955 by the Armstrong Whitworth company. Although it was designed as a private venture civilian freighter, in the end, it was the Royal Air Force that operated the most of this type.

Initially named 'Freightliner', in July 1958 it was given the same name as an earlier success from Armstrong Whitworth, the 1926 three-engined Argosy airliner. Later in life it was nicknamed the 'Whistling Wheelbarrow' on account of the twin-boomed layout and distinctive engine noise. Construction of ten aircraft was commenced at Bitteswell after market research had shown significant interest from the airlines.

Thanks in part to the time saving use of drawings and components which were already in production as well as the subcontracting of the design and building of various units, it took only 23 months from the final drawings being produced to the first flight on the 8th January 1959. It may seem remarkable that the wings of the Argosy were based on those fitted to the Avro Shackleton Mk.3 but it is more obvious that the engine nacelles were copied from the Vickers Viscount. The Gloster Aircraft Company were contracted to build the tail unit and they also designed the 'Rolamat' cargo handling system.

The first order came in 1959 from the Miami-based freight airline Riddle Airlines, but it was not until April 1961 that BEA announced an order for three aircraft to replace Yorks and Dakotas on their European freight services. These were the only airlines to order new Argosies from the manufacturer.

The first Argosy designed for the military was the AW.660 (later Hawker Siddeley HS.660). This had extra fuselage doors for paratrooping, a completely new 'clamshell' style rear door with an integral loading ramp and a nose-mounted radar that necessitated the sealing-up of the large nose-doors. The first of 56 RAF Argosy C.1s entered service in 1962. After service, most of these were broken up at Kemble in the mid-70s but a few were sold to civil operators.

The Argosy Series 200 was first flown on 9th March 1964. This had wider front and rear doors, an enlarged freight hold and a new, lighter, fail-safe wing. BEA part exchanged their three Series 102s and bought five of the new version, known as the Series 222. These entered service in February 1965 but were not considered a success and were retired in April 1970.

Second hand sales over the years saw the survivors of the 73 Argosies built operating in Australia, Canada, Gabon, Ireland, New Zealand, the Philippines and the Democratic Republic of Congo. Among the last operators were: Air Bridge Carriers, Elan Air, IPEC

Aviation and Safe Air; however it was Duncan Aviation in Alaska who operated the last flying Argosies in the world in the autumn of 1991. Three of their aircraft still exist; one (the prototype Argosy) is at the Yankee Air Museum in Detroit, another is preserved amongst the fire bombers at Fox Field in California and the other at the Mid America Air Museum in Sioux City, Iowa. This last one was dismantled into manageable pieces in 1999 and flown from Nebraska to Iowa slung beneath a US Army CH-47 helicopter. In the UK, preserved examples are at the Cosford Aerospace Museum, the Midland Air Museum in Coventry and the East Midlands Aero Park.

Specifications (for the Series 200)

Span: 35.05m (115ft 0in)
Length: 26.44m (86ft 9in)
Engines: Four 1,663kW (2,230shp) Rolls-Royce Dart 532/1 turboprops
Cruise speed: 435 km/h (235kts)
Payload: 14,095kg (31,080lb) optional 89 passengers

Originally operated by Riddle Airlines in the USA, this Argosy 101 of BBA Cargo was seen at its Melbourne-Essendon base in September 1974. Note the vortex generators behind the cockpit that alter the airflow along the fuselage. (Author's collection)

One of six Argosies still in existence is the second one built, G-APRL. Seen here at Cologne in 1985, 'Edna' was preserved at the Midland Air Museum at Coventry airport in 1987. (Author's collection)

One of three Ansett operated Carvairs, VH-INK was delivered to Australia in November 1965. This magnificent shot shows 'November Kilo' at Melbourne-Tullamarine in March 1973. (Author's collection)

AVIATION TRADERS ATL98 CARVAIR

Aviation Traders (Engineering) Ltd
Southend Airport, Essex
England

In the 1950s, the British travelling public were becoming far more adventurous and airlines such as Silver City and Channel Air Bridge were busy flying passengers and their cars on Bristol Freighters (see page 50) on the short hop across the English Channel to mainland Europe. As the demand for this operation grew, Channel Air Bridge's associate company, Aviation Traders, initiated designs for a larger aircraft able to carry more cars and passengers further into Europe.

Due to the prohibitive costs in building a small production run of a large new passenger/car transport, the Aviation Traders designers planned their aircraft around the conversion of the readily available and inexpensive Douglas DC-4/C-54 Skymaster (see page 82). To test and prove their conversion ideas, various fuselage shapes were 'flown' in the Cranfield wind tunnel. Subsequently, a nose mock-up was made at Southend followed by actual conversion work on an Air Charter C-54B in October 1960. The entire fuselage forward of the wing was removed and replaced by one 2.64m (8ft 8in) longer, built to Douglas production standards. The all-important direct entry for vehicles was achieved by raising the cockpit 2.08m (6ft 10in) and by making the nose wheel retract into a fairing. The hydraulically operated sideways-opening nose door allowed vehicles to be driven in after they had been raised to the floor level by a scissor-jack. An enlarged

DC-7 tail fin was fitted as compensation for the extra side area and to give greater rudder control. The brakes were also upgraded by using DC-6 components. Up to 25 passengers could be carried in the standard five-abreast rear cabin, although the aircraft could be converted to full passenger configuration carrying 85. The winner of a local naming competition invented the name 'Carvair', derived from 'car via air'.

First flight was on 21st June 1961 and over the next seven years, 21 Carvairs were built with deliveries to Aer Lingus, Ansett-ANA, Aviaco, British United Airways and Interocean. BUA had been formed in July 1960 from the merger of various concerns including Airwork, Channel Air Bridge, Air Charter and Hunting-Clan, however they initially operated Carvairs in Channel Air Bridge colours.

Strong competition from the cross-channel ferries eventually saw the surviving British Carvairs used more and more as pure freighters. By the mid 1980s, about seven Carvairs were still in existence but only a handful were flying with freight operators such as Academy Airlines, Gifford Aviation and Pacific Air Express.

In 1999 the only operator of a Carvair was Terrace, British Colombia-based Hawkair Aviation Services. Their immaculate example is employed alongside a Bristol Freighter (see page 50) carrying cargo to and from a remote gold mine in Canada. In Georgia, another

Carvair is about to enter service with Custom Air Service. Stored or derelict examples exist at Wonderboom in South Africa and in the Democratic Republic of Congo.

Specifications

Span: 35.82m (117ft 6in)
Length: 31.27m (102ft 7in)
Engines: Four 1,080kW (1,450hp)
    Pratt & Whitney R-2000 Twin Wasp
    radial pistons
Cruise speed: 334km/h (180kts)
Accommodation: 85 passengers or
    5 cars plus 25 pax

This is British Air Ferries' Carvair G-ASKN 'Big Bill' about to land on runway 06 at Southend airport in May 1976. It was sold in the Gabon in 1976. (Author's collection)

The only operator of the Carvair in 1999 was British Colombia-based Hawkair. They acquired C-GAAH in May 1997 for work at a gold mine but the recent closure of the mine has prompted them to offer the aircraft for sale. (Dario Cocco)

Delivered new to British South American Airways Corporation in 1946, York 1 G-AHFB 'Star Stream' survived later service with BOAC, Skyways and Arab Airways before succumbing to the breaker's axe at Luton in 1963. (Harry Holmes Collection)

AVRO 685 YORK

A V Roe and Co Ltd
Newton Heath, Manchester
England

In the mid-1930s, Boeing used the wings, undercarriage and tail of their B-17 Flying Fortress and mated them to a new fuselage to create the Boeing Stratoliner (see page 36). Similarly in England, but several years later, the wings, undercarriage and tail of the famous Lancaster bomber were joined to a new fuselage design to create the Avro York.

The first York was constructed in six months at Chadderton after Avro had received approval to build a prototype from the British Air Staff. Prior to the first flight in July 1942, discussions with BOAC regarding their preferred powerplant led to the third York being built in full passenger configuration with air-cooled Bristol Hercules radial engines instead of the liquid-cooled Merlins. The Royal Air Force ordered 200 aircraft, without knowing which engine would be fitted, but after a series of trials, the Merlin engine was chosen. Handling trials were flown at Boscombe Down where the test pilots found some directional instability, but this was rectified by addition of a central fin.

A total of 256 Yorks were built, with the last one being delivered to the RAF in 1948. Several versions were produced, including some well-known VIP examples that were used by Winston Churchill, King George VI and Earl Mountbatten. The early civil operators were BOAC, Skyways Ltd, British South American Airways Corporation and FAMA of Argentina.

The York is famous for its use in Operation Plainfare, the Berlin airlift. RAF and Skyways' Yorks flew supply missions between Wunsdorf and Gatow, often carrying more than 7,400kg (16,500lb) of dusty coal. Thanks to the low fuselage door, a turnround of 40-45 minutes could be achieved. The RAF Yorks were operated by 241 OCU and 24, 40, 51, 59, 99, 206, 242 and 511 Squadrons. The only civilian York operator on the airlift was Skyways. They used three Yorks, one of them flying 1,298 hours during 480 sorties as a freighter and as a tanker.

In the 1950's and 60's, various airlines made use of the York, both as passenger airliners and as freighters. These included Dan-Air Services, Hunting-Clan Air Transport, Trans Mediterranean Airways, Middle East Airlines, Persian Air Services, Air Liban and Maritime Central Airways. The RAF retired their last York in 1957. The last ever York service was with Dan-Air London's G-ANTK on 30th of April 1964.

At least two examples of this historic aircraft have survived. Dan-Air's G-ANTK, for many years used as a scout hut at Lasham airfield in Hampshire, was donated to the Duxford Aviation Society in 1986 and is now under restoration to static display condition at the Imperial War Museum at Duxford. This mammoth task is proceeding slowly and final completion is planned for 2006. A former Skyways York, G-AGNV, is preserved in full

RAF markings at the Cosford Aerospace Museum. Substantial parts of a York are also believed to still exist where it crashed in Canada in the 1950's.

Specifications

Span: 31.09m (102ft 0in)
Length: 23.92m (78ft 6in)
Engines: Four 1,215kW (1,610hp) Rolls-Royce Merlin 502 piston engines
Cruise speed: 404 km/h (251 mph)
Accommodation: 12-65 passengers
Payload: 14,307kg (31,542lb)

A foggy February morning at Heathrow in 1964 found Skyways venerable York G-AGNV waiting for its next load. This aircraft is currently preserved in RAF colours at Cosford. (Author's collection)

RAF York C.1 MW232 was bought by Dan-Air Services in 1954. It operated for ten years before retiring to Lasham where it was used by Lasham Air Scouts as a bunkhouse. Seen at Duxford, it is undergoing restoration to static conditions. (Author)

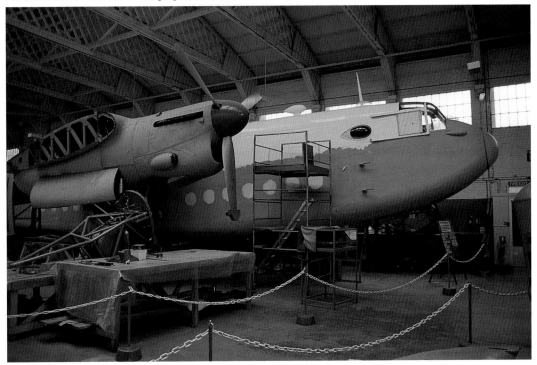

G-ARAY, the second Avro 748, was originally built as Series 1 but was converted to a Series 2 in 1961. In April 1965 it was photographed about to depart Woodford for a lease to Leeward Islands Air Transport. (Harry Holmes)

BAe 748 AND HAL 748

British Aerospace, Woodford, Cheshire, England.
Hindustan Aeronautics Ltd, Chakeri, Kanpur
India

In 1957 the British government boldly forecast that there would be no more manned military aircraft. A V Roe and Co Ltd, who were heavily involved in the production of military aircraft, therefore decided to re-enter the commercial market with a DC-3 replacement. Their proposed design of a high-wing, twin-engined 20-seater powered by Rolls-Royce Dart turboprops was rejected by the airlines who preferred a low-wing aircraft with a sturdy undercarriage, easy maintenance and a cabin clear of obstruction from the wing spar. Avro listened to the airlines and later offered a slightly larger 36-seater of conventional design with the designation Avro 748.

The prototype first flew from Woodford in June 1960 as a Series 1 with 1,400kW (1,880ehp) Darts. The flight was noteworthy because, at 2 hours 41 minutes, it was the world's longest first flight by a new civil airliner.

A month before the first flight, the Indian government signed an agreement with Avro allowing the 748 to be assembled from British-built components by Hindustan Aircraft Ltd at Kanpur. The first of 89 Indian-built examples flew in November 1961 and last one was completed in 1984. All were delivered to either the Indian Air Force or to Indian Airlines.

Skyways Coach Air and Aerolineas Argentinas made the first scheduled

commercial services with a 748 in April 1962. Overseas sales were gained after the company demonstrator flew a vigorous and successful worldwide sales tour. In 1963/64 the aircraft flew more than 91,000 miles on sales tours to Europe, Africa, India, the Far East, the Caribbean, South America and Canada. At around this time, Hawker Siddeley Aviation Ltd absorbed Avro, thus causing the re-naming of the aircraft as the HS.748.

Development of an uprated Series 2 commenced very early in the programme. In 1961 the second prototype Series 1 was converted into the first Series 2 with more powerful Mk.531 engines and increased weights and range. The Dart 7 Mk.532-powered HS.748 Series 2A first appeared in 1967 and was ordered by the Brazilian airline VARIG.

In 1962, a competition was held at Martlesham Heath between a Handley Page Dart Herald (see page 100), and the second prototype 748 for a manned (government change of mind!) military freighter. The sturdy 748 was successful and the RAF ordered 31 examples of a much-modified version, the Avro 780. These were delivered from 1965 and had a rear loading ramp, 'kneeling' undercarriage and additional strengthening. In RAF service these aircraft became the Andover C.1, and since their retirement, several of these rugged freighters have found use with civilian operators particularly in

Africa. The Andover name was also applied to other military HS.748s including the two specially equipped aircraft supplied to the Queen's Flight.

In April 1977 the 748 came under the British Aerospace banner and continued to be marketed as the BAe 748. The aircraft was further updated as the Series 2B, with more power, an increased wing span and a modified tail. The last version produced, the Super 748, first flew in July 1984 and was similar to the 2B, but with a completely updated flightdeck and cabin, and quieter engines. The last 748 built was delivered to Makung Airlines in Taiwan in January 1989.

About 100 are in current use, many of them as freighters. The type, which has become universally and affectionately known as the 'budgie' over the years, is still popular with Canadian operators but the largest fleet is operated in the UK by Liverpool-based Emerald Airways.

Specifications

Span: (2A) 30.02m (8ft 6in)
   (Super) 31.23m (102ft 6in)
Length: (2A & Super) 20.42m (67ft 0in)
Engines: Two 1,700kW (2,280ehp) Rolls-Royce
   Dart RDa.7Mk.534-2, or 535-2, or 552-2
Cruise speed: 452km/h (244kts) max
Accommodation: 58 maximum

Only nine 748s were operated in the USA. This is N749LL on its delivery flight to Air Illinois at London Gatwick in December 1980. This aircraft is currently in service with Executive Aerospace in South Africa. (Author)

A new HS.748 operator in Europe is Gothenburg-based West Air Sweden. They have 11 'Budgies' including Series 2A SE-LIA that was originally delivered to Rousseau Aviation. (Avimage)

LANICA (Lineas Aereas de Nicaragua) had four BAC 1-11s. Series 412 AN-BBI was delivered to Managua in 1967 and returned to Hurn airport for maintenance where it was photographed in June 1972. (Author's collection)

BAe (BAC) ONE-ELEVEN

British Aerospace, Woodford, Cheshire, England
Romaero, Bucharest, Romania

The British Aerospace One-Eleven, or BAC 1-11 as it is still called, can trace its lineage back to the 1956 Hunting Aircraft H.107 design for a 32-seat Viscount replacement, powered by two Bristol Orpheus turbojets. Several years of dithering and design changes meant that the eventual BAC 1-11 layout did not however appear until April 1961.

The final design, complete with a clean wing, tail cone mounted APU, ventral air-stair and Rolls-Royce Spey engines, soon attracted interest from the airlines. British United Airways were first with an order for 10 aircraft; more significant however, were the orders from the USA. Braniff International Airways, American Airlines, Mohawk Airlines and Aloha Airlines all ordered the unflown airliner straight from the drawing board.

The prototype was first flown from Hurn Airport as a Series 200 with Rolls-Royce Spey 506 engines on 20th August 1963. Two months later it crashed. The accident was attributed to a phenomenon known as a 'deep stall', from which recovery was virtually impossible. The crash caused severe delays to the 1-11 programme but after leading edge wing modifications and powered elevators had been fitted, the 1-11 had no further problems. It is interesting to note that BAC provided Douglas with information gleaned from the accident regarding the behaviour of 'T' tail twinjets. Douglas, who were finishing design work on their DC-9, said thanks very

much and promptly modified the wing and tail of their new airliner.

The identically sized Series 300 and 400 were heavier and faster and were powered by the Spey Mk.511. In January 1967 BEA ordered 18 of the 97-seat Series 500 which was specifically designed for BEA for use on their extensive European routes. The Series 500 was created by stretching the fuselage with a 2.54m (8ft 4in) fuselage plug forward of the wing, and another plug 1.57m (5ft 2in) behind the wing. The span was increased by 1.52m (5ft 0in) and a strengthened undercarriage and Spey Mk.512 engines were fitted.

The last British built example of the One-Eleven was the Series 475. This had the short fuselage of the Series 200/300/400 and the wings and engines of the 500. Designed for use at 'hot and high' airports such as those found in South America, only 12 were built including a 1-11 Series 487GK(F) freighter delivered to TAROM.

In 1981, the entire One-Eleven production was transferred to Romaero SA in Bucharest. The first Romanian-assembled ROMBAC 1-11 Series 560 flew in September 1982 and all nine examples were delivered to the Romanian national airline, TAROM.

With the arrival of the Stage 2/Chapter 2 noise restrictions, many of the 1-11s still flying in the 1980s were treated with 'hushkits'. This allowed continued use of the type, but Stage 3/Chapter 3 restrictions will

ground many 1-11s in the Western world unless they can find new owners elsewhere or their operators can justify the further expense of Stage 3 hushkits.

The 1990s witnessed a 1-11 revival. Bournemouth-based European Aviation is now the world leader in 1-11 technology and maintains the largest fleet of the type anywhere. A Stage 3/Chapter 3 hushkit for the Rolls-Royce Spey engine has been developed in partnership with Quiet Technologies of Florida, leading to a European Airlines 1-11 appearing at the 1998 Farnborough Air Show complete with the modified engine.

More than 100 BAe 1-11s are currently in service worldwide, with Africa now the home to many of them thanks to the lenient noise regimes in places like Nigeria and the Republic of South Africa. Small fleets operate in Indonesia and Pakistan and a few survive as executive jets in the USA while in Europe, TAROM, British World and EAL still operate significant fleets. The only preserved examples appear to be in the UK at Duxford, Brooklands and Cosford.

Specifications (for a Series 500)

Span: 28.5m (93ft 6in)
Length: 32.6m (107ft 0in)
Engines: Two 55.8kN (12,500lb)
     Rolls-Royce Spey 512DW turbofans
Cruise speed: 851km/h (470kts)
Accommodation: 119 maximum

Taxying on to the South Pier at London Gatwick airport in June 1997 is European Aviation's BAC 1-11 Series 510ED G-AVMT. They leased the aircraft to Air Bristol who sub-leased it to AB Shannon. (Author)

South Africa currently has a large fleet of BAC 1-11s in service. Nationwide Airlines' hushkitted Series 537GF ZS-NUI displays its 'Right Whale' colour scheme in October 1998. (African Aviation Slide Service)

This is Howard Hughes' specially constructed Boeing Stratoliner N19904 'The Flying Penthouse' at Fort Lauderdale in 1964. The fuselage of this aircraft is still in Florida, converted into a houseboat. (Jay Miller Collection)

BOEING 307 STRATOLINER

Boeing Aircraft Company
Seattle, Washington
USA

Due to the ever-increasing advances in technology in the 1930s, aircraft manufacturers were able to announce that their latest commercial airliner had something new in its design that was going to significantly change the future for the airlines and their passengers. Whether it was retractable undercarriage, de-icing equipment or onboard lavatories, they all demonstrated the progress in airliner design. The outstanding concept in the Boeing 307 Stratoliner was that it was pressurised.

In 1940, it became the world's first pressurised airliner to enter service, allowing it to fly 'above the weather' and thereby provide a smooth flight for its passengers. Despite this notable and historic achievement, the Stratoliner was a financial flop for the Boeing Company, and only ten examples were built.

Designed in the mid-1930s, the Model 307 was based on the famous B-17 Flying Fortress bomber and had the same basic wing, undercarriage, engines and tail unit. As was the fashion in those days, the all-new circular cross section fuselage could be converted from a 33 passenger 'day-time' layout, to a 'night-time' configuration, with accommodation for 25 passengers, (16 in sleeper berths, and 9 in comfortable reclining chairs)

Initial interest from both Transcontinental and Western Air (later TWA) and Pan

American, secured orders and options for 29 aircraft. However, most of these were cancelled, leaving most American fare-paying passengers to fly in such types as the reliable, but unsophisticated, Douglas DC-3 and DST.

Deliveries to the two airlines commenced in 1940. Pan Am based their three Stratoliners in Miami for services to Brazil, while TWA concentrated their five examples on the lucrative New York-Los Angeles run. One famous Stratoliner (N19904) was delivered to Howard Hughes in July 1939 for an abortive 'round the world' record-breaking trip. This low-time aircraft was wrecked in a hurricane in Florida but the surviving fuselage was ingeniously converted into a luxury houseboat, still retaining many of the cabin and cockpit fittings.

In 1951, TWA sold their fleet to the French airline, Aigle Azur. After Aigle Azur was taken over by UAT in 1955, the Stratoliners remained in the Far East, and in 1964 a handful were operating charters around Saigon and Hanoi. Amazingly, some of these Stratoliners were still operating 'diplomatic flights' in Laos in 1974.

Surviving examples include the 'Howard Hughes' houseboat in Fort Lauderdale, Florida, and N19903. This had originally been delivered to Pan American in May 1940 as 'Clipper Flying Cloud'. After service in South Africa, it was sold to the Haiti Air Force in

1954 for use as a VIP transport, but was sold back to the USA in 1957. Remarkably, this historic aircraft survived and was eventually bought by the National Air & Space Museum in Washington. They loaned it to the Pima Air and Space Museum in Arizona until Boeing paid for it to be restored to flying condition prior to flying it to Seattle in May 1994. This aircraft, currently at Seattle under the care of Boeing, will eventually be displayed, together with the prototype Boeing 707, at a new NASM Annexe at Dulles International Airport. It is believed to be the only complete example of a Stratoliner in existence, I say, 'believed', because intriguing rumours still circulate about a Stratoliner still surviving in a hangar somewhere in Laos!

Specifications

Span: 32.69m (107ft 3in)
Length: 22.65m (74ft 4in)
Engines: (307) Four 820kW (1,100hp) Wright Cyclone GR-1820-G102 piston engines (SA307-B1) Four 895kW (1,200hp) Wright Cyclone GR-1820-G666 piston engines
Max cruise speed: 355km/h (222mph)
Accommodation: 38 maximum

Royal Air Lao acquired the ex TWA and Aigle Azur Stratoliner XW-TFP in the 1970s. If rumours can be believed, this aircraft may still exist in a hangar 'somewhere' in SE Asia. (Author's Collection)

Restored to airworthiness after resting for several years at the Pima Air Museum, Stratoliner N19903 flew to Washington in 1994 where it undergoing a full restoration. (Bob Shane)

This fantastic photo was taken around 1950. Boeing 377-10-34 Stratocruiser N31225 was the first United Airlines aircraft delivered in September 1949. It was sold to BOAC in 1954 as G-ANTX. (Boeing Company Archives)

BOEING 377 STRATOCRUISER

Boeing Aircraft Company
Seattle, Washington
USA

During the dark days of the Second World War, Boeing commenced design studies to test the feasibility of building a transport version of the Boeing B-29 Superfortress. Impressed with the idea, the USAAF ordered three prototypes to be built in January 1943. Using the same idea that created the Stratoliner (see page 36) from the B-17, Boeing built a new pressurised upper fuselage and mated this to as many B-29 parts as possible. Because the wings, lower fuselage, empennage, engines and undercarriage all came from the giant bomber, the time taken to complete the prototypes was greatly reduced. The impressive result was the huge 'double-bubble' fuselage Model 367, known to the military as the YC-97 'Stratofreighter'.

Boeing also saw the potential for a civil airliner based on the YC-97, but detail work on this had to wait until VJ-Day before Boeing could spare design staff. Using a YC-97B as a basis, they built the prototype Boeing Model 377 'Stratocruiser' and this first flew on the 8th July 1947.

Pan American became the first to order the Model 377, eventually operating the largest fleet of 27. Other orders came from American Overseas Airlines, BOAC, Northwest Orient Airlines, Transocean Airlines, United Airlines and Scandinavian Air Lines (later cancelled).

Like the later Boeing jetliners, the Strato-cruiser series carried various model numbers that related to the ordering airline and their particular equipment requests. Pan American's model 377-10-26 Stratocruisers were eventually flown with either 61 seats for daytime passengers or 27 night berths plus 25 seated.

In 1958, Transocean Airlines had four converted to a high-density 117-seat arrangement. Despite its bulbous nose and huge girth, the Stratocruiser had a longer range and was faster than the Constellation, and with its spiral staircase leading down to the lower deck lounge/cocktail bar, it was very popular with the passengers. The only downside apparently was the reliability of the complex Wasp Major engines. Not generally realised is that all Model 377s had a foldable tail fin to allow entry into low hangars. Northwest's and United's aircraft had square passenger windows.

After a series of proving flights, the first true revenue earning flight by a Pan Am Stratocruiser was on April 1st 1949, followed by BOAC on 6th December 1949. By the late 1950s, the arrival of the jet-powered Comet and Boeing 707 saw the Strats gradually withdrawn and sold off to operators including RANSA in Venezuela and the Israeli Air Force.

Several civil-registered Model 367 Stratofreighters survive, but all of the 56 civil Stratocruisers built between 1947 and 1949 have gone. The world's last true complete 'Stratocruiser', as opposed to a civilianised C-97, was broken up at Tucson in 1984.

However, it would be unfair to exclude this classic airliner from this book because of the visual similarity between the two types. Plenty of the 850+ military Model 367s (C-97 Stratofreighter) still survive, some of them having served in civil airline operations, and most of the converted 'Guppy' Stratocruisers also exist (see page 8).

Mention should be made of the efforts by the Berlin Airlift Historical Foundation to get an ex USAF Stratofreighter into the air. In October 1998 they flew C-97G N117GA 'Deliverance' from Moses Lake in Washington State to Greybull, Wyoming for restoration. The Strat, although due to be completed in military markings, will hopefully show airshow visitors some of the grandeur of the missing Stratocruisers.

Specifications

Span: 43.05m (141ft 3in)
Length: 33.63m (110ft 4in)
Engines: Four 2,610kW (3,500hp) Pratt & Whitney R-4360-TSB3-G Wasp Major Radial pistons
Cruise speed: 547 km/h (340mph)
Accommodation: 89-112

Photographed in Mexico in 1989, XA-PII was named 'La Paz' after its base city. Originally built in 1953 as a C-97G for the USAF, this aircraft still exists at Tucson Airport. (Pierre-Alain Petit)

This ex-USAF C-97 Stratofreighter was used by the Red Cross organisation for relief work in Africa. It is currently preserved at the magnificent Pima Air Museum in Arizona. (Author)

Note the early engine exhaust outlets on this 707-328 of Air France. F-BHSK was delivered to Paris in 1960 and apart from a lease period to Air Madagascar, it remained in French service until retired in 1977. (Brian Stainer)

BOEING 707

Boeing Commercial Airplane Group
PO Box 3707, Seattle, Washington
98124-2207, USA

Now undoubtedly considered a classic jet airliner, the Boeing 707 was a privately funded venture conceived in the 1950s as a jet powered military tanker for the USAF, but with a potential for production as an airliner. Boeing's Model 367-80, popularly known as the 'Dash Eighty', first flew in July 1954. This prototype became the Boeing 707, an airliner that became synonymous with jet air travel for the 1960s. In October 1954, the first order for the 707 was for 29 of the military tanker/ transport version known as the KC-135A Stratotanker. A year later, the first civil order for 20 aircraft was accepted from Pan American. Once Pan Am had taken this leap towards a jet fleet, other major airlines were compelled to keep up by ordering their own jet-powered fleets of 707s or the rival Douglas DC-8, and orders snowballed.

In order to satisfy the requirements of the various customers, Boeing offered a number of different variants of the 707. Initially these were a short or long-bodied 707-120 and the more powerful 707-220. The short fuselage/long range series 120 (similar in length to the Boeing 720, see page 42) was only ordered by the Australian airline Qantas. In October 1959, the Qantas 707s were the first to operate a round-the-world jet service. The short-to-medium range 130-seat Boeing 720 is covered separately on pages 42-43.

The longer fuselage 'Intercontinental' series 320 first flew in January 1959 and was ordered by Air France, Pan Am, Sabena and TWA. An order from BOAC specified their series 320 should have Rolls-Royce Conway engines and they appeared with the designation 707-420. These aircraft were the first 707s to be fitted with the taller (by 2ft 11in) fins and the ventral underfin that were subsequently fitted to all new 707s and retrofitted to many early 707s and 720s. Conway-powered 707-420s were also ordered by Air India, El Al Israel Airlines, Lufthansa and Varig.

The availability of the more efficient turbofan engine created the most popular versions of the 707, the Series 320B and C. These models can be distinguished by their new, bigger front cowling and their slotted leading edge flaps. First flown February 1963, the 707-320C was a convertible passenger/ cargo variant with a large 2.31m x 3.40m (7ft 7in x 11ft 2in) forward freight door, it is the most common type of 707 still flying today.

Almost all of the approximately 100 surviving airworthy 707s are Series 320B or C. Many of these will be banned from Europe and the USA in the year 2000 unless their engines have been 'hushkitted' to Stage 3 noise limits. Omega Air/Tracor is one partnership that offers the alternative of re-engining; they can fit a 707 with Stage 3 compliant JT8D engines for about $16 million per aircraft, half the price that the USAF spent to re-engine their KC-135s with CFM56s.

Even after the Stage 3 noise restrictions are enforced, many JT3D-powered 707s will still find work in the Middle East, Africa and some Central and South American countries that are unconcerned about environmental noise pollution.

In addition to airworthy examples of this historic jetliner, many others can be found stored and dumped worldwide. The very first 'Dash Eighty' was presented to the National Air and Space Museum (part of the Smithsonian Institution) in 1972 and it is currently stored at Boeing Field in Seattle. Other preserved civil 707s can be found in Berlin, Brussels, Cosford, Damascus, Paris and Tucson.

Specifications

Span: 120B - 39.90m (130ft 10in)
    320B - 44.42m (145ft 9in)
Length: 120B - 44.07m (144ft 6in)
    320B - 46.60m (152ft 11in)
Engines: 120B - Four 76.2kN (17,000lb)
    P&W JT3D-1 turbofans
    320B - Four 80kN (18,000lb) P&W JT3D-3 or
    84.4kN (19,000) P&W JT3D-7 turbofans
Cruise speed: 120B - 1,000kmh (540kts) max
    320B - 974km/h (525kts) maximum
Accommodation: 120B - 179 maximum
    320B - 219 maximum
Freighter payload: 40,000kg (88,900lb)

In 1984 it was still possible to see passenger-carrying 707s in Europe. A set of steps to climb and some nice afternoon sunshine made this shot of Worldwide Airlines N8733 at Gatwick all the better. (Author)

Seen at Sharjah in March 1998 is Nairobi-based African Airlines International's Boeing 707-330B 5Y-AXI. This, now rare, 164-passenger aircraft was previously operated by Air Zimbabwe. (Author)

This early Braniff scheme, also used on their BAC 1-11s, may not be as colourful as Braniff's later offerings, but this late 1960s shot of B720-027 N7077 is certainly very fine. (Erik Bernhard collection)

BOEING 720

Boeing Commercial Airplane Group
PO Box 3707, Seattle, Washington
98124-2207, USA

The short to medium range Boeing 720 airliner (initially referred to as the Boeing 717) was designed for the US domestic market. Officially launched in July 1957, the type obtained its first order in November when United Airlines ordered 11 Boeing 720-022s with a further 18 on option.

Compared to the 707, the fuselage was to be 2.36m (7ft 9in) shorter than the standard model 100 and was based on the short-bodied Boeing 707-138 being built for Qantas of Australia. Higher speeds and better performance than the 'Intercontinental' 707 were achieved by the provision of a smaller fuel capacity, a revised inboard wing profile and a lighter wing structure and engines. The standard 707 tailfin used on the 720 was later increased in height by 0.96m (3ft 2in) and several 720s were retrofitted with it. An increase over the 707's cruise speed by Mach 0.02 to Mach 0.90 allowed the 720 to compete with the Convair jetliners (see pages 62 and 64) and, thanks to the full-span leading edge flaps, the 720 could operate from airfields with short runways. The large amount of commonality between the 707 and 720 allowed airlines with a mixed 707/720 fleet to make significant savings on spares holdings and crew training.

The prototype Boeing 720 first flew at Renton on 23rd November 1959. With three aircraft used by Boeing for test flights, the certification was completed by June 1960.

The first Boeing 720 service was Chicago-Denver-Los Angeles flown by United Airlines on 5th July 1960. Apart from United, early operators of the 720 were American Airlines, Irish International Airlines, Braniff International Airways, Eastern Air Lines and Pacific Northern Airlines.

With the arrival of the higher-powered and more fuel-efficient JT3D turbofan engines, Boeing could re-engine existing 720s and manufacture new examples. This version, the Boeing 720B, first flew in October 1960 and orders were obtained from American, Avianca, Continental, El Al, Ethiopian, Lufthansa, Northwest Orient, Pakistan International, Saudia, TWA and Western International. 65 non-fan (eleven later converted to 720B) and 89 fan-powered 720s were completed by 1967 with the last one being delivered to Western Air Lines in September. The last airline to operate 720s was probably MEA who still had two in service in 1994.

Of the 13 Boeing 720s believed to survive, only two are thought to fly on a regular basis. Pratt & Whitney Canada use an ex-MEA example at Montreal as a flying testbed for engines, and Sheikh Kamal Adham of Saudi Arabia has used another as an executive jet since 1978. Pratt & Whitney also have two stored in Mojave for reserve/spares alongside another that is used by Raytheon for US government work. Garrett Turbines have one as a static engine testbed at Phoenix, Arizona.

Preserved examples can be found in Taiwan, Colombia, Korea and Pakistan, while some still earn their keep as cabin trainers and instructional airframes. Another old MEA 720 was in use as a restaurant in Beirut in 1995.

Specifications

Span: 39.88m (130ft 10in)
Length: 41.68m (136ft 2in)
Engines: (720) Four 54.3kN(12,000lb) or
 57.8kN (13,000lb) Pratt & Whitney JT3C-7
 or -12 turbojets
 (720B) Four 75.6kN (17,000lb) Pratt & Whitney
 JT3D-1 turbofans
Cruise speed: 896 km/h (484 kts)
Accommodation: 131 (156 in 720B)

About to land on runway 28L at Heathrow in November 1977 is Boeing 720-051B G-AZFB. This aircraft was leased to Cyprus Airways by Monarch Airlines who operated three Boeing 720s. (Author)

This 1961 vintage Boeing 720-023B C-FETB has been used as an airborne test-bed by Pratt & Whitney Canada for 15 years. Note the PW150 turboprop on the nose and the roof panel which dissipates electrical energy produced by the test engine. (Pratt & Whitney Canada)

This photograph shows Boeing 737-247 N4525W of Western Air Lines one week after it had been delivered in April 1969. The aircraft later served with Frontier Airlines and Continental Air Lines. (Author's collection)

BOEING 737-100/200

Boeing Commercial Airplane Group
PO Box 3707 Seattle, Washington 98124-2207
USA

Around 1962, Boeing began design studies for a new small regional jet that would complement their existing range of jet airliners. When the Boeing 737 was officially launched in November 1964, it was offered with seats for 60-85 passengers in a fuselage that was about 85ft long, however, discussions with Lufthansa, the original customer, persuaded Boeing to offer a larger version seating 100. By February 1965 Lufthansa was satisfied with the design and ordered 21 Boeing 737 Series 100 to replace their Viscounts and ConvairLiners on their European network. Two months later, United Airlines ordered 40 with options for a further 30, but unlike Lufthansa they specified the proposed larger version, the Series 200.

To save production costs and to give the airlines valuable commonality of parts, many systems and components of the earlier Boeing jets, particularly the 727, were utilised. These included the passenger doors, cabin furnishings, the engines and significantly, the fuselage cross-section.

First flight of what was to become the world's best selling jetliner was in April 1967 at Boeing Field in Seattle. The short-bodied Series 100 proved unpopular in comparison with the Series 200 and only 30 were built for Lufthansa, Malaysia-Singapore Airlines and Avianca Colombia. One airline that still operates a couple of the Series 100 is Aero Continente in Peru.

The first of 248 Series 200s flew in August 1967 and both the 100 and 200 Series were granted FAA certification in December. United Airlines flew the first service with a 200 in April 1968. In 1970, the production line moved to Renton and in 1971 the Series 200 was replaced by the Series 200 'Advanced'. These had a new automatic brake system, more efficient thrust reversers in longer engine nacelles as well as various structural and aerodynamic improvements.

Over 100 Series 200s were completed as 200C (Convertible) and 200QC (Quick-Change) versions. These had a 2.18m (7ft 2in) by 3.40m (11ft 2in) cargo door, and a strengthened cabin floor. Boeing brochures reported that an experienced crew could convert the 200C to freight layout in 57 minutes, but thanks to its 'palletised' passenger seats, the QC could be stripped of seats and be ready for freight in 11 minutes!

A total of 865 of the 'Advanced' Series 200 were delivered to operators worldwide by the time production stopped in 1988. By this time the CFM56-powered Series 300 had been flying for nearly four years and no further orders for the outdated Series 200Adv had appeared. The last of the JT8D-powered 737s was delivered to CAAC of China in August 1988. About 130 Series 200/200C/200QC still fly airline services in addition to over 750 of the 200Advanced. Currently Delta Airlines and US Airways operate the largest fleets of JT8D-powered 737s. Many of these have had their engines 'hushkitted' by firms such as Nordam in order to conform to Stage 3/ Chapter 3 noise restrictions.

Despite the huge numbers of late model and new generation 737s that have been built, Boeing's original baby jet can still be found in service with several major airlines including Aerolineas Argentinas, Air France, Air New Zealand, British Airways, Canadian, Sabena, Saudi Arabian Airlines and Varig. Early models in good condition and with airframe hours remaining can still find buyers and now that the new airlines in the FSU are able to choose their aircraft, they are quite happy to operate a 30-year old 737-200 in preference to a younger Tupolev jet.

Despite the availability of many early 737s which have been withdrawn for scrapping or 'parting out', it is really quite surprising that only one civil Boeing 737 has been preserved. Aircraft number 1, originally registered N73700, is currently stored awaiting its place at the Museum of Flight in Washington.

Specifications

Span: 28.35m (93ft 0in)
Length: 737-100 28.65m (94ft 0in)
  737-200 30.48m (100ft)
Engines: Two 62.7kN (14,000lb) to 77.4kN
  (17,400lb) Pratt & Whitney JT8D turbofans
Cruise speed: 917km/h (495kts)
Accommodation: 737-100 115, 737-200 130,
  737-200Adv 125 maximum

Photographed on its delivery flight to New Zealand in October 1978 is Boeing 737-219 ZK-NAR. The aircraft remained with Air New Zealand until 1994 when it was sold to TACA. (Author's collection)

Love them or hate them, British Airways' 'ethnic' tail colours at least provided a bit of variety compared to the awful all-over white scheme that is now prevalent. This is 737-236(Advanced) G-BGDE in Sterntaler colours at Gatwick in 1998. (Author)

Compare this Braniff colour scheme to the one featured on the Boeing 720! Boeing 747-127 N601BN was delivered to Braniff in January 1971 and, not surprisingly, each of their similarly painted small fleet of jumbos were known as the Big Orange. (Author's collection)

BOEING 747-100/200

Boeing Commercial Airplane Group
PO Box 3707, Seattle, Washington 98124-2207
USA

Without doubt, the Boeing 747 'Jumbo Jet' has proved to be the most significant aircraft of the 1970s. With its huge increase in capacity compared to the then current airliners and the reduction in operating costs bought about by its economy of scale, the 747 brought affordable long range travel to the world's airline passengers. Many of these early versions have now become too expensive to maintain and are being retired, stripped for spares reclamation and the remainder sent for scrap. However, more than 100 of the Series 100 and 350 Series 200s are still in service more than 30 years after the first flight. The Jumbo is definitely a Classic airliner, indeed, many airline crews in the older three-crew mechanical cockpit variants report their aircraft type to Air Traffic Control using the name 'classic' to differentiate them from the later, two-crew EFIS-equipped 747s.

In the mid 1960s, the Boeing Company was competing with Lockheed and Douglas for a contract to build and supply a fleet of very large strategic jet transport aircraft for the USAF. The contract was won by Lockheed with their C-5 Galaxy, but Boeing's efforts were not wasted as they were able to use their design as a basis for a new civil airliner. Early Boeing drawings showed a two-deck 'double-bubble' fuselage with seven-abreast seating and two aisles. This layout was firmly rejected by the airlines and the design was altered into what was essentially an overgrown Boeing

707. The new fuselage was designed with a single passenger deck and two aisles seating ten across and, unique among jet airliners but 'old hat' to the designers of the Carvair (see page 28), a cockpit positioned on a separate floor above the main deck with a small cabin lounge area behind.

Pan American World Airways placed a letter of intent for 25 aircraft with Boeing in December 1965 and by September 1966, Boeing had obtained orders for 56 747s from seven airlines including Air France, BOAC, Lufthansa, JAL and TWA. By the time the prototype first flew at Everett, in February 1969, the 747 order book had grown to 160 aircraft for 27 airlines. FAA Type Approval was granted in December 1969, and Pan Am flew the first transatlantic New York-London 747 service in January 1970.

Boeing announced the 747B version in November 1967. This had extra fuel capacity and a revised undercarriage allowing for operation at higher weights. This was later given the designation 747-200, leaving the original as the -100. The basic Series 100 was only available with Pratt & Whitney engines but later models had the option of the Rolls-Royce RB-211 or General Electric CF6 engines.

Although a pure cargo 747 was planned from the start, a 747F did not appear until Lufthansa's first example flew in November 1971. This had a hinged nose that swung

upwards to permit direct entry/exit of pallets or freight. The 747C 'Convertible' (also with the hinged nose) first flew in March 1973 and was first delivered to World Airways. The 747 'Combi', normally built without the hinged nose because it had a large rear cargo door, was first delivered to Sabena in 1974.

In 1973, Boeing introduced the 747-100B (SR) (Short range). This was designed specifically for the high-density, short-haul market in Japan, where a few are still in service configured for over 530 passengers. A couple of Series 100B (SR) with a stretched upper deck are also in service with JAL with 563 seats!

Currently the largest fleets of Series 100s are operated by All Nippon, British Airways, Polar Air Cargo and UPS. The more popular Series 200 operates with airlines all over the world but none have found buyers in the FSU. Many early 747-100s still exist, including the prototype that will no doubt be preserved. Considering its bulk and scrap value it is hardly surprising that no 747s are currently preserved for public display.

Specifications (for the 747-100)

Span: 59.64m (195ft 8in)
Length: 70.66m (231ft 10in)
Engines: Four 207kN (46,500lb) GE CF6-45A2 or 208.9kN (46,950lb) P&W JT9D-7A or 213.5kN (48,000lb) P&W JT9D-7F
Cruise speed: 965km/h (522kts) maximum
Accommodation: 500 maximum

A dramatic dark sky enhances this shot of All Nippon's Boeing 747-281B JA-8190 at Gatwick in 1989. Note the small (probably 10ft long!) sticker on the nose advertising the Japanese Expo 90 exposition. (Author)

Many wide-bodied jets including the Boeing 747, DC-10, TriStar and A300 are now finding new markets as freighters after withdrawal from front line passenger service. This ex-Singapore 747-212B was seen at Ontario airport in California in May 1998. (Author)

This much-published photograph of Breguet Universal F-BASV was taken at Heathrow south side in March 1967, two years after the type was placed in regular service between London and Paris. (Brian Stainer)

BREGUET BR 761/763/765

Société Anonyme des Ateliers d'Aviation Louis Breguet, Toulouse, France

The Breguet Br 761 Deux Ponts (two decks) was the first of a series of short/medium range transport aircraft, designed originally in 1944 for either passengers or freight, which included the Br 763 and Br 765. The prototype Br 761 was constructed at Villacoublay with 1,178kW (1,580hp) SNECMA-built Gnome-Rhone 14R radial engines and first flew on 15th February 1949. A pre-production batch of three Br 761S models were then built with a few modifications including a centre tail-fin, modified wingtips and the more powerful 1,506kW (2,020hp) P & W R-2800-B31 engines.

Satisfactory flight tests failed to prompt any early orders from the biggest potential buyer Air France. However one Br 761S was leased to Air Algérie and operated in full airline livery, and another, F-BASL, was leased for three months in 1953 by the British airline Silver City Airways Ltd, who based theirs in Berlin, replacing Bristol 170s on the freight service to Hamburg. Altogether the Silver City Deux Ponts made 127 round trips carrying a maximum of 127,000lbs of cargo.

Air France eventually showed interest and ordered 12 of the improved Br 763 Provence, which first flew in July 1951. The Br 763 had strengthened wings with a longer span and a cockpit reconfigured for three crew rather than the earlier four. Air France received their first Br 763 in August 1952 and the type was

placed in regular service on the Lyons-Algiers service in March 1953. In 1964, six Air France Br 763s were transferred to the French Armée de l'Air in the Pacific and given the type name 'Sahara'. The remaining six Air France Provences were reconfigured as convertible cargo/passenger/vehicle transports and given the new name 'Universal'. These conversions were made partly because of the need for an aircraft that could transport the Bristol Siddeley Olympus engines from the UK to France for Concorde production. Internal modifications included the provision of a winch and a massive lift for manoeuvring heavy freight to the upper deck. Maximum payload in the Universal became 13,150kg (28,990lb). Optional loads included freight plus 20-29 seats on the forward upper deck or up to 12 small cars. The last Universal was withdrawn in March 1971.

The final version was the Br 765 Sahara that first flew on 6th July 1958. The four Br 765s, all delivered to the French military, could carry 146 fully equipped troops or 85 casualties on stretchers. Other loads included a 15-ton AMX tank, a 105mm field gun battery or 17 tons of mixed freight. The Sahara had removable clamshell doors under the rear fuselage and it could also be fitted with large wing tip fuel tanks for extra range.

I was very fortunate to witness a few of the Air France freight flights operated by the converted Universals at Heathrow in the

1960s. Amongst the aircraft enthusiasts, they were still referred to as the Deux Ponts and their noisy departures and appalling rate of climb have endeared the type to me for many years!

Three examples are believed to survive in France. The Aero Club at Fontenay-Tresigny, 40km east of Paris has a genuine, ex-Air France Br 763 and Evreux Aero Club is believed to have a Br 763 in poor condition. Br 765 'Sahara' No.504 is preserved by Ailes Anciennes at Toulouse-Blagnac. This aircraft, 'Brigitte', was dismantled at Evreux in Normandy in 1985 and transported piece by piece by road to Toulouse where the last section eventually arrived in 1987. It is currently undergoing restoration to static condition in full Air France colours.

Specifications

Span: 42.99m (141ft 0in)
Length: 28.94m (94ft 11½in)
Engines: Four 1,790kW (2,400hp)
    Pratt & Whitney R-2800-CA18 piston radials
Cruise speed: 351 km/h (281 mph)
Accommodation: 59 upper deck, 48 lower deck, or 135 in high-density layout
Payload 12,228kg (26,960lb)

Action shots of this rare aircraft are hard to find. This is Air France's F-BASQ roaring onto finals for runway 28R at Heathrow Airport in May 1968. (Frank Tyler)

The Deux Ponts was never an elegant beast, and the addition of concrete pillars and fake propellers has made this example look even more cumbersome. Originally delivered to Air France, F-BASS was later sold to the French Air Force and now serves as a bar/restaurant at Fontenay-Tresigny. (Peter Marson)

The beautiful light on this shot shows Aer Turas' 'Biffo' EI-APM on the south side parking area at London Heathrow in February 1967. This aircraft crashed at Dublin four months later. (Author's collection)

BRISTOL 170 FREIGHTER/SUPERFREIGHTER/WAYFARER

Bristol Aeroplane Co Ltd
Filton, Bristol
England

Design work on this famous workhorse began during the Second World War. The Bristol Aeroplane Company proposed their type 170 as a rugged freight carrier with a large forward clamshell door in the aircraft nose. The simple structure, incorporating a strong fixed undercarriage, Bristol Perseus engines, and a declared ease of maintenance, enabled Bristol to offer the 170 at an economical price, and ensured that its operating costs would be low.

Because of the early interest shown in the type by the British military, the design was enlarged to enable it to carry a 3-ton Army truck. However, the two prototypes constructed were not to military specifications because the RAF's interest in the 170 had diminished at the end of the war.

Bristol decided to launch the 170 on to the civilian market with a choice of interiors and functions. Initially, a Series I Freighter with the nose doors, and a Series II passenger version (known as the Wayfarer) without the nose doors, were offered to airlines and air forces. Successful flight trials followed the first flight which was made from Filton in December 1945. Subsequently, several long-distance demonstration tours showed off the Freighter's capabilities and led to orders from all over the world.

Two, very famous, 'cross-channel' Bristol 170 Freighter services were operated on opposite sides of the world. From 1948, Silver City Airways flew services from Lympne and

Lydd in Kent to Le Touquet in France, while in New Zealand, Safe Air's large fleet of Bristol Freighters made the hop over the Cook Strait, between the North and South islands, from 1951 until the last one was withdrawn in 1988. For their services to the Chatham Islands, Safe Air designed a special passenger capsule that was fitted out as the inside of an airliner, complete with windows. The capsule was loaded into the Freighter through the front doors, changing the aircraft to an airliner in a matter of minutes.

The Mk.32 Superfreighter, first seen in 1953, has now disappeared completely. This version had a larger, revised tail fin and an extended nose allowing the carriage of three cars plus 20 passengers.

The Bristol 170 was immensely strong but it could often live up to its nickname 'Frightener' because of its ability to collect ice. The thick wing with its poor de-icing equipment and the bulbous nose were ideal aerial ice collectors and caused many headaches for its aircrew.

Three years ago there were two Freighters flying but one of these sadly crashed at Enstone in the UK in July 1996. At the time of writing, the only Bristol 170 in flying condition is in Canada. Until the middle of 1999, Hawkair Aviation Services of Terrace, British Colombia, used their 'Biffo' and an equally rare ATL.98 Carvair for freight services to remote gold mining sites. Amid harsh

conditions these two veterans brought in supplies and returned to civilisation with the bags of mined material. Hawkair's unique fleet now awaits new tasks but if nothing is forthcoming, they may have to be sold.

Preserved Freighters can be found at Yellowknife and Winnipeg in Canada; Wangaratta and Point Cook in Australia; Blenheim, Founders Park, Wakapuaka, Waihi and Wigram in New Zealand and at Buenos Aires-Newberry in Argentina.

Specifications (for a Mk.31)

Span: 32.92m (108ft 0in)
Length: 20.83m (68ft 4in)
Engines: Two 1,476kW (1,980 hp) Bristol Hercules 734 piston radials
Cruise speed: 262km/h (165mph)
Accommodation: 15 to 23 passengers

Hercules Airline's Bristol Freighter ZK-EPD was originally delivered to the Royal New Zealand Air Force in 1952. After a couple of years in the UK, it was sold to Canada in 1987 as C-GYQS as shown in the photo below.(Chris Mak)

Until the middle of 1999, the world's last airworthy 'Biffo' C-GYQS flew regular support missions to a remote gold mine in the NWT. Now that the contract has finished, hopefully some new work can soon be found for this remarkable aircraft. (Avimage)

Photographed at Heathrow in the early 1960s, Canadian Pacific's Britannia CF-CZC became G-ATLE in 1965 and survived as a training airframe at Gatwick for many years before succumbing to the scrapman in 1984. (Author's collection)

BRISTOL TYPE 175 BRITANNIA

Bristol Aircraft Ltd, Filton House, Bristol, England and Short Brothers & Harland Ltd Queen's Island, Belfast, Northern Ireland

The wartime Brabazon committee was responsible for the birth of many classic British-built aircraft including the Ambassador, Comet, Viscount and Dove. In 1944 their recommendations included a request for a 'Type 3' design for a medium-range 30-passenger airliner for post-war use by BOAC. One of the ten manufacturers to offer designs for this potentially prestigious airliner was the Bristol Aircraft Company with their 36-seat Type 175 powered by four Bristol Centaurus piston radial engines. The Ministry of Supply ordered three Centaurus-powered prototypes, but when the Proteus turboprop became available, the MoS changed their order allowing two to be built with the new turboprop engines leaving the third to be used as a design mock-up.

In July 1949 BOAC formally ordered a fleet of 25 of the new Bristol airliner. Strangely, their order specified 6 with piston engines and 19 with turboprops. The capacity of the Type 175 was soon increased to 64, and after a successful series of air tests with a Proteus grafted on to an Avro Lincoln flying test-bed, BOAC amended their order and the piston-powered version was dropped. An idea of what a piston-powered 'Brit' would have looked like can be had by looking at a Canadair Argus.

In 1952, the Type 175 was christened 'Britannia', and test pilot Bill Pegg first flew the prototype at Filton on 16th August, one

month before the airliner made its first public appearance at the Farnborough Air Show. Despite the certification process suffering serious delays due to the overstressing of the first prototype and the forced landing of the second, several major airlines ordered the Britannia, particularly the stretched Series 300. These included Aeronaves de Mexico, Capital Airlines, Northeast Airlines, Cubana, Canadian Pacific, Trans Continental SA, El Al, Ghana Airways, Hunting-Clan and Air Charter (London). The subsequent cancellation of contracts, due to financing problems, by Northeast and Capital meant that no Britannias were ever sold in the USA.

The three basic versions of the Britannia were given the series numbers 100, 250 and 300, with each customer's specific models identified by the addition of further numbers. For example, BOAC's first Britannias were Series 102 and Cubana's were Series 318. The only series 100s were the short-fuselage prototype 101s and BOAC's fleet of 102s. The stretched-fuselage (3.12m/10ft 3in) Series 250 was intended to be a civilian freighter with a large forward freight door, but no civil orders were forthcoming and the only versions completed were as Series 252 and 253 for use by the Royal Air Force. In RAF service these Britannia C.1 and C.2s had cabins convertible between an all-freight mode and one with 99 rearward-facing seats for trooping. The Series 300, originally

designed for BOAC transatlantic operations, evolved into the definitive long-fuselage passenger transport. All versions were popularly called 'Whispering Giants'.

An early example of political correctness affected one of BOAC's Britannias. After Series 102 G-ANBG had suffered some technical problems, it was re-registered G-APLL in 1958. The reason? BOAC's engineers had nicknamed the aircraft 'No Bloody Good'!

Despite the fact that only a few, non-flying, examples exist, the Britannia's name will live on for many years. When the British airline Euravia bought five, ex-BOAC, Series 102s in 1964, they adopted the airliner's name for themselves; since then, Britannia Airways has become Britain's largest charter airline.

Five Britannias survive in the UK, while a few others may still exist as wrecks in Cuba and the Democratic Republic of Congo. The museums at Duxford and Cosford have one each, while Kemble has the world's only taxiable Brit as well as one in pieces. The Luton Airport Fire Service still uses a fuselage for training.

Specifications (for a Series 312)

Span: 43.36m (142ft 3in)
Length: 37.87m (124ft 3in)
Engines: Four 3,072 ekW (4,120 ehp)
Bristol Proteus 755 turboprops
Cruise speed: 575 km/h (355 mph)
Accommodation: 139 (maximum)

BOAC's Britannia 102 G-ANBO was delivered in 1957. It was later operated by Luton-based Britannia Airways from 1965 to 1970. It is seen here at Manchester in April 1969. (Author's collection)

Well travelled Britannia 312 G-AOVF saw service in the UK with BOAC, British Eagle, Monarch, Donaldson, IAS, Invicta and Redcoat. It has been preserved at Cosford since 1984. (Author)

Trans Canada Airlines received DC-4M2 North Star CF-TFB from Canadair in October 1947. Ten years later it was converted to a freighter and eventually ended her days in Mexico as XA-NUU. (Air Canada Archives)

CANADAIR DC-4M NORTH STAR
Canadair Limited
Cartierville, Montreal
Canada

The North Star was conceived around 1944 as a pressurised, Merlin-powered, version of the Douglas C-54 Skymaster (see page 82). With the end of the war in prospect, Trans-Canada Airlines anticipated the need to replace their ageing fleet of passenger-configured Avro Lancasters and made exhaustive studies into the airliner types that would be available from the British and American manufacturers. They concluded that because of its strength, simplicity and reliability, the ideal airliner for construction in Canada would be the Douglas C-54/DC-4. A brand new company, Canadair, was formed to build the new airliner using the best available engines and equipment.

A great deal of discussion took place regarding the type of powerplant for the new airliner and it was eventually decided that a new, more powerful, Rolls-Royce Merlin liquid cooled engine would be preferable to the air-cooled Pratt & Whitney radials that were fitted to the C-54/DC-4.

With perfect timing for Canadair, Douglas were about to sell-off their C-54 production line at Parkridge in Illinois, complete with more than 60 unfinished fuselages. A deal was therefore agreed with the Canadians whereby Douglas would sell Canadair the parts, and also assist in the redesign and production of a Merlin-powered DC-4 airliner.

However, the DC-4 lacked one major item that was essential for Canadian air travel,

pressurisation. Douglas's engineers re-designed the fuselage to allow pressurisation and in addition permitted Canadair to adapt various items from their new DC-6 including the undercarriage and flaps.

The first DC-4M North Star flew from Cartierville in July 1946, and deliveries commenced to Trans Canada Airlines and the Royal Canadian Air Force. In 1948, Canadian Pacific Airlines ordered four aircraft, and BOAC ordered 22, to be known as the Canadair C-4 'Argonaut'.

Due to the licence restrictions placed by Douglas, only Canada and the UK ordered new North Stars. This restricted the production run to only 71 aircraft. At first, the new airliner was not popular with its passengers due to the deafeningly loud roar from the inboard Merlins. Modified 'cross-over' exhaust outlets were eventually fitted which reduced the cabin noise to a more bearable level.

By the 1960s, the North Star/Argonaut fleets of the major airlines were removed from front line service and sold to various smaller independent operators, many of them based in Europe providing scheduled and inclusive tour (IT) charter services. British operators included Gatwick based Overseas Aviation who operated a fleet of 16, Derby Airways (later British Midland) with 3 and Air Links (Transglobe) who had 4. Outside the UK, Flying Enterprise, Aden Airways and East

African Airways all operated ex-BOAC Argonauts.

There is only one confirmed survivor of this type. An RCAF North Star is preserved at the National Aviation Museum at Rockcliffe Airport, Ottawa. The famous North Star that was the 'Wings' restaurant for many years in Mexico City was cut up in July 1993 after an onboard fire, though the nose is now reportedly preserved in a technical museum. The last airworthy North Star was grounded on Greater Inagua Island near Cuba in 1979. It may still be there!

Specifications (for the C-4 'Argonaut')

Span: 35.80m (117ft 6in)
Length: 28.60m (93ft 7½in)
Engines: Four 1,305kW (1,760hp) Rolls-Royce Merlin 624 or 724-C1 V12 piston
Cruise speed: 523km/h (283kts)
Accommodation: 54 (Maximum 78)

Seen at Rome airport in the early 1950s, BOAC's C-4 Argonaut G-ALHF 'Atlas' was bought by East African Airways Corporation in 1957 as VP-KOI. Note the flags in the cockpit windows and the precarious job that the BP man has with overwing refuelling in the rain. (Jay Miller collection)

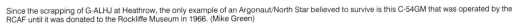

Since the scrapping of G-ALHJ at Heathrow, the only example of an Argonaut/North Star believed to survive is this C-54GM that was operated by the RCAF until it was donated to the Rockliffe Museum in 1966. (Mike Green)

One of two ex-British CL-44D4s operated by Sion-based freight airline Transvalair was HB-IEO. This view taken at Palma in August 1978 shows the two hinge fairings on the rear fuselage to advantage. (Author's collection)

CANADAIR CL-44 & YUKON

Canadair, Cartierville Airport
St Laurent, Montreal
Canada

In the early 1950s, the Royal Canadian Air Force (RCAF) produced a requirement for a maritime reconnaissance and anti-submarine patrol aircraft which would be based on the Bristol Britannia (see page 52) and licence built in Canada. The result was the CL-28, known to the RCAF as the CP-107 Argus. Apart from the Wright Cyclone piston engines, tail boom and the modified nose, the Argus was externally very similar to the Britannia. The RCAF received their first Argus in 1957.

Around the same time, Canadair proposed yet another Britannia variant to fulfil the RCAF requirement for a pressurised long-range troop and freight transport to replace their fleet of Lancasters. The result was the CL-44. Twelve aircraft, known by the RCAF as the CC-106 Yukon were ordered, with the original intention of fitting Bristol Orion turboprops. Prior to the completion of the design, the Orion engine was abandoned, thereby forcing Canadair to use the lower powered Tyne.

Using their experience with the Argus, Canadair built the CL-44/CC-106 Yukon with a longer, pressurised, fuselage, greater wing-span and strengthened undercarriage. Two large freight doors were provided forward and aft of the wing on the port side to allow freight and pallets to be loaded efficiently.

While the Yukons were under construction, Canadair engineers, encouraged by US cargo airlines, Seaboard & Western and Flying Tiger Line, carried out a major re-design of the rear

fuselage and tail, deleting the rear cargo door and creating a 'swing tail' CL-44D4. This version could be identified by the two large hinge covers on the rear starboard fuselage and the revised cockpit windows. The Yukon used the same cockpit windows as the Britannia, but due to American certification problems regarding cockpit visibility, all the other CL-44s were completed using the window design from the Convair 880/990 airliner (see pages 62-64). The first CC-106 Yukon flew on 15th November 1959, followed a year later by the first CL-44D4.

In May 1959, Seaboard and Western (later Seaboard World) ordered five CL-44D4s, and Flying Tigers ordered ten. Later, another US freight airline, Slick Airways ordered four. Known in civilian life simply as the 'Forty-Four', the type proved successful in service but only 27 were built.

Three CL-44D4s were used by the Icelandic airline Loftleidir for cheap transatlantic passenger services. In order to squeeze in more passengers, Loftleidir ordered a fourth to be built with a stretched (4.62m/15ft 2in) fuselage seating 214; this version was known as the CL-44J or Canadair 400. Pleased with their new money-spinner, Loftleidir had their other CL-44D4s converted to 'J' standard.

The RCAF retired their Yukons in 1973 and all 12 were sold to civilian operators, mostly in South America. Most of the D4s and Js survived into the 1980s having been flown by

operators in countries including Colombia, Cyprus, Ecuador, Great Britain, Ireland, Libya, Switzerland, the USA and Zaire.

One Flying Tiger D4 was converted by Jack Conroy Aviation for outsize loads, particularly Rolls-Royce RB-211 engines for the Lockheed TriStar. The unique CL-44-0 'Guppy' which first flew in November 1969, retained its swing-tail but had its entire upper fuselage replaced to create a cavernous hold 3.45m (11ft 4in) high and 4.24m (13ft 11in) wide. In early 2000, this aircraft was in Smyrna, TN awaiting a new engine prior to re-entering service in March at Ostend with First International Airlines.

It is doubtful if any examples of the Yukon survive; however, there is a chance that surviving remnants of a few are at Kinshasa and at Goma. The CL-44 can definitely still be found in the Democratic Republic of the Congo (formerly Zaire), where Africargo, who also trade with the names Trans Lloyd Cargo and Professional Aviation are reported to have a couple in service, but up to date news from this country is hard to come by.

Specifications (for a CL-44D4)

Span: 43.37m (142ft 4in)
Length: 41.73m (136ft 11in)
Engines: Four 4,276kW(5,730shp)
Rolls-Royce Tyne 515/50 turboprops
Cruise speed: 621km/h (335kts)
Accommodation: 134 to 178 (214 in CL-44J)
Payload: 29,959kg (66,048lb)

The similarity of the CC-106 Yukon to its predecessor, the Britannia, is revealed by the cockpit windows. Compare them to Convair-style windows on the CL-44. 9Q-CWK was seen in store at Manston in April 1982. (Author)

Seen at Sharjah in November 1997, Liberian registered CL-44D EL-WLL was once a common sight in the UK. Transmeridian Air Cargo, British Air Ferries and Heavylift were all previous operators of this 1961 freighter. (NARA)

Ethiopian Air Lines operated three Convair 240s. ET-T-20 was delivered to Addis Ababa in December 1950 where it served for 14 years before being sold in the USA; it was converted to Rolls-Royce Dart power in 1966. (San Diego Aerospace Museum)

CONVAIR 240/340/440

Consolidated Vultee Aircraft Corp
San Diego, California
USA

In 1945, American Airlines asked various manufacturers to submit their designs for a DC-3 replacement. San Diego-based Convair offered a neat twin-engined tricycle undercarriage 30-passenger airliner with the designation Convair 110. The unpressurised CV-110 first flew on 8th July 1946 and although it performed successfully, the type had already been rejected by American as being too small for their operations and only one was built. However, the prospective customers encouraged Convair to use the 110 as a basis for a larger airliner.

Using the same basic layout and powerplants but with a longer and slimmer pressurised fuselage, Convair built their model 240 (2 from the number of engines, 40 from the number of seats) and after a successful first flight on 16th March 1947, American placed a huge order for 75 aircraft. Powered by 1490kW (2000hp) Double Wasp engines, the CV-240, later called the Convair-Liner, became the world's first pressurised twin-engined airliner, and despite the huge numbers of cheap ex-military Douglas C-47s available to the civil market, many major airlines placed orders for the new aircraft. These included Continental, FAMA Argentina, KLM, Pan American, Swissair, TAA Australia and Western. The CV-240 remained in production until 1958, by which time 176 civil and 395 military versions (C-131 & T-29) had been built.

A further increase of capacity was offered in 1951 when Convair revealed their 44-seater Model 340. Changes to the basic CV-240 design consisted of new 1790kW (2400hp) engines, a 1.36m (4ft 6in) fuselage stretch, a 4.14m (13ft 7in) increase in wing span with more fuel space, a new undercarriage, revised flaps and a new cabin interior. The first one flew in October 1951 and 55 of the type were swiftly ordered by United Airlines who cancelled a large order for the Martin 3-0-3. United commenced CV-340 services in November 1952. In total, 133 civil CV-340s and 99 military C-131/R4Ys were built.

Prompted by the competition from the Vickers Viscount, Convair upgraded the 340 into the 440 and gave it the name Metropolitan. Standard interior was still 44; however a 52-seat interior was optional, as was a nose-mounted weather radar. Many of the 153 CV-440s built were operated in Europe where they competed with the Vickers Viscount. European orders were obtained from Alitalia, Iberia, Lufthansa, Sabena, SAS and Swissair.

Almost half of the total piston Convair-Liner production was converted to turboprop power between 1955 and 1967 (see page 60) and it is those that have continued to find employment especially in Canada and the USA. The few surviving airworthy piston-engined Convair-Liners are confined mostly to freight operations in places such as Bolivia,

Mexico, the USA, Haiti and the Dominican Republic. At the time of writing, the only European commercial operation of a piston-powered Convair-Liner is the Evora-based Portuguese company Agroar, who use their 1957-built Metropolitan and an equally smart turboprop Convair 580 for freight services. However, this immaculate machine has reportedly been acquired by the British airline Air Atlantique at Coventry.

Over 100 piston Convair-Liners exist worldwide, but most of them are either stored or preserved. The largest group consist of retired military C-131s and T-29s in museums in America; other preserved examples of the civil 240/340/440 series can be found in Brazil, China, Egypt, Finland, Japan, Norway, Paraguay, Philippines, Serbia and Thailand.

Specifications (for the Convair 440)

Span: 32.12m (105ft 4in)
Length: 24.84m (81ft 6in)
Engines: Two 1,865kW (2,500hp) Pratt & Whitney R2800-CB16 or 17 Double Wasp radial piston
Cruise speed: 483kmh (261kts) maximum
Accommodation: 52 maximum
Payload: 5,820kg (12,836lb)

Convair 240-0 N74850 was delivered to American Airlines in June 1948 and in 1960 it was bought by Fort Worth-based Central Airlines. Converted to a Series 600 in 1966, it still flies to Fort Worth with its current owner Kitty Hawk Air Cargo. (Jay Miller Collection)

Near the picturesque town of Evora in Portugal is the base of Agroar. Apart from a fleet of Agcats and an Islander, they operated two Convair-Liners including CS-TML, the very last piston-powered Convair-Liner to be commercially operated in Europe. (Author)

This unique aircraft is the Convair 240-21 Allison Turbo-Liner N24501. Powered by Allison T-38 engines, in 1950 it was the only turboprop Convair-Liner. It was later de-converted to regular piston power. (San Diego Aerospace Museum)

CONVAIR 540/580/600/640 & 5800

All aircraft built originally by Convair, and converted to turboprop power by D Napier and Sons, Canadair, PacAero or Convair

The first efforts at converting the widely used Convair-Liner to turboprop power commenced in 1949 when the prototype Convair 240 was fitted with Allison T-38 turboprops and christened the 'Turbo-Liner'. Despite considerable interest from airlines and especially the US military, the converted aircraft was not particularly relevant for operational use due to the engine's lack of development. However, this work provided valuable data for the later conversions which used the advanced version of the T-38, the Allison T-56 (501) engine. The US military test flew two T-56-powered Convair YC-131Cs in 1954, but declined to order the type in quantity for the USAF. In September 1957, civil certification of the T-56 as the Allison 501-D13 allowed its use in the Lockheed L-188 Electra and the later Convair 580 conversions.

In 1954, the British aero engine manufacturer, D Napier and Sons saw the potential for re-engined Convair-Liners in commercial use. In December that year, they obtained a nearly new CV340 from America and replaced the Pratt & Whitney piston engines with their own 2,280kW (3,000hp) N.El.1 'Eland' engines. This high quality conversion first flew at Luton, England in February 1956. Initially known as the Napier Eland Convair, the aircraft was later known as the Convair 540. A second example was converted by Pacific Airmotive for use as a

demonstrator and for certification in the USA. Allegheny Airlines flew the demonstrator under service conditions and were impressed enough to order five aircraft. Ten further Eland-powered Convairs were built from new by the Canadair Company for the Royal Canadian Air Force. These were designated CL-66 by Canadair and CC-109 by the RCAF.

The most popular Convair-Liner conversion, the 580, was the result of an agreement by Convair with PacAero Engineering Corp of Santa Monica in California. Convair were busy with their Model 880, so they appointed PacAero (already experienced in converting one aircraft to Eland power) to become the official 'converter' for all Convair 340/440s to Allison power. The first 'Allison Super Convair' flew at Santa Monica in January 1960 and after entering airline service the designation Convair 580 was allocated. Altogether 175 CV340/440s were converted to Convair 580 layout. More than 100 remain in service; British Colombia-based Kelowna Flightcraft currently operate the largest fleet.

Having completed design work on their Models 880 and 990, Convair investigated a scheme where they could re-engine Convair-Liners using a lower-powered turboprop than the Allison, that would suit the Convair 240 as well as the 340/440s. The popular Rolls-Royce Dart 542-4 engine was chosen and the first conversion flew in May 1965. Convair 240s

with Darts became CV-600s, and 340s and 440s became CV-640s. From the 38 CV240s and 27 CV340/440s that were converted to Dart power, about 25 are still in service; the largest fleet is operated by Kitty Hawk Air Cargo in Dallas, Texas.

Apart from operating the largest 580 fleet, Kelowna Flightcraft also completed the most dramatic Convair-Liner conversions. They dismantled a Convair 580 and stretched the fuselage by 4.25m (13ft 11in). The resulting CV-5800 first flew in February 1992. Powered by two Allison 501-D22G turboprops and seating up to 78 passengers, the Convair 5800 was widely promoted but only two were completed and both are currently in use as freighters. One is with Contract Air Cargo at Oakland, Michigan.

Recent interest in preserving the airliner heritage of the USA in flying condition has prompted the acquisition of various types. The Mid Atlantic Air Museum have now obtained a Convair 580 which belonged to Forbes Magazine. This aircraft will be restored in Allegheny colours to fly alongside their Viscount and Martinliner.

Specifications (for the Convair 580)

Span: 32.12m (105ft 4in)
Length: 24.84m (81ft 6in)
Engines: Two 2,800kW (3,750shp)
    Allison 501-D13H turboprops
Cruise speed: 550km/h (297kts)
Accommodation: 56

Originally a Convair 340 with the Arabian American Oil Company, this aircraft was converted to a 440 and later a 640. C-FCWE was photographed at Tucson in the colours of short-lived Canada West Air in March 1990. (Author)

Seen here at Merida in February 1999, Air Venezuela's Convair 580 YV-970C was originally a Convair 340 delivered to Philippine Airlines. It was converted to Allison power while owned by North Central Airlines in 1969. (Chris Mak)

N8802E 'Delta Queen' was the first Convair 880 to be delivered to Delta Air Lines in 1960. Converted to freight configuration in 1978, it was destroyed by fire in Mexico in 1983. (San Diego Aerospace Museum)

CONVAIR 880 AND 880M

General Dynamics Corporation
San Diego, California
USA

Despite their eventual reliability and some airline successes, the two Convair jetliners described in this book caused a commercial disaster for their manufacturer and forced them to withdraw from the civil market. The production run of only 102 Convair 880s and 990s, together with various manufacturing delays, high operating costs and management and customer altercations, brought about a $425 million loss for General Dynamics.

When it was first proposed, the 'Eight-Eighty' was known as the Skylark 600. Later designation changes to Golden Arrow and Convair 600 were also dropped in favour of Convair 880. The number 880 was reportedly chosen because it was the design's cruise speed, expressed in feet per second!

With the objective of a large order from TWA, General Dynamics proposed their new high-speed jet airliner in 1956. With potential competition from Douglas and Boeing in the long-haul market, GD chose a narrow five-abreast fuselage with a 35 degree swept wing designed for a 600-mph cruise on medium to long range.

The strongly built Convair 880 airliner had a couple of features that easily distinguished it from the Boeing and Douglas opposition. A long thin fairing on top of the fuselage covered the VHF aerials and the ADF antennae, much like some Soviet built airliners. It also had unique 'wedge' shape passenger doors which were also used on the 990 (see page 64).

At the time of the first flight, from Lindbergh Field, San Diego on 27th January 1959, commercial interest in the 880 was poor. In order to attract more customers, the 880M (M for modified) was offered with improved wing-lift devices, more powerful engines and a new centre fuel tank. The 880M first flew in October 1960, but the competition from Boeing and Douglas was too strong and only 48 standard and 17 'M's were completed.

The largest fleet was operated by TWA with 28, followed by Delta Air Lines with 17. Delta operated 880s from 1960 until they were part-exchanged for Boeing 727-200s in 1973. Other major operators included Cathay Pacific, Japan Air Lines, KLM, Northeast Airlines and VIASA.

After retirement from front line operations, several 880s were converted to freight configuration with the addition of a large forward cargo door and a strengthened floor. Most of these were operated in Central and South America but they had all been withdrawn by the mid-1980s.

The 880 was not a common sight in Europe, but you can still find one today near Lisbon Airport. N8806E was abandoned at Lisbon Airport in 1980 and later converted into a restaurant. This enterprise has since failed, but the old Delta Air Lines ship still survives. More than 15 still exist in the USA, most of them in long-term storage at Mojave. Probably the most famous surviving 880 is

the one preserved at Graceland in Tennessee. Elvis Presley bought the ex Delta Air Lines aircraft for $1m in 1975, named it after his daughter and used it until his death in 1977. The 'TCB' and lightning bolt on the tail signify 'Taking Care of Business in a flash'!

The last 880 to fly, in December 1995, was the US Navy's unique UC-880. Multiple uses for this much-modified ex FAA bird included in-flight refuelling and chasing cruise missiles!

Specifications (for a model 880)

Span: 36.58m (120ft 0in)
Length: 39.42m (129ft 4in)
Engines: Four 51.8kN (11,200lb)
General Electric CJ-805-3 turbojets
Cruise speed: 990km/h (615mph)
Accommodation: 88 to 110 (maximum124)

Another old Delta Convair 880 which was converted to a freighter was N8816E. Operated by Latin Carga as YV-145C, it was photographed at Miami in September 1980, two months before it was written of in a crash at Caracas. (Author's collection)

Elvis Presley was the most famous private owner of an 880. He purchased this ex-Delta Air Lines example in 1975 and named it after his daughter, Lisa Marie. The 'TCB' on the tail stands for 'Taking Care of Business'. The aircraft is currently preserved at the Graceland Museum. (Author's collection)

Immaculate line-up of three of the eight Swissair Coronados at Zurich in 1972. After retirement, HB-ICC was transported by barge in 1975 to the Swiss Transport Museum on the lakeside at Lucerne, where it is still on display alongside a Swissair DC-3. (Bernard King)

CONVAIR 990 AND 990A

General Dynamics Corporation
San Diego, California
USA

With the sales of the Convair 880 (see page 62) at such a poor level, General Dynamics tried very hard to improve its sales potential by re-engineering it into a much modified 'new' airliner, the Convair 600.

In those days, the airlines competed with each other on matters such as speed, comfort and range. With new, higher powered and more efficient GE turbofan engines, the proposed airliner would certainly be faster than any other; indeed GD virtually guaranteed a 635 mph maximum cruise speed. Comfort would not be a problem; many passengers had already discovered the advantages of the five-abreast seating in the 880, and the 600 would not be any different. The 2.74m (9ft 6in) fuselage stretch allowed up to 98 first class seats in four-abreast, or a maximum of 137 in a high density five-abreast arrangement. The one item that could not be guaranteed until the aircraft was in service was range. GD hoped that the advertised 4,400-mile range could actually be achieved and that the total package would encourage the operators, particularly American Airlines, to place orders.

In August 1958 American Airlines did order 25 Convair 600s, but before the first one took to the air in January 1962, GD changed the name to Convair 990 to demonstrate that it was a newer model than the 880. The 990 was later given the name 'Coronado' by Swissair.

The 880's dorsal fairing and strangely-shaped passenger doors were still in evidence, but the most obvious difference to its predecessor were the four 'speed pods' on the wing trailing edge. These were anti-shock bodies, designed to alter the position of the drag inducing shock wave that could actually reduce the wing efficiency near to Mach 1. The fact that they could be used as additional fuel tanks was an added bonus. The 990 also broke ground by being the first jet airliner to have anti-skid brakes.

Although it was fast, the 990 embarrassed GD by failing to achieve its design speeds. Significant modifications were needed to the engine nacelles, wing leading edge and the fuselage/wing fairings before the maximum cruise speed of 1,000km/h (621mph) was attained. Thus modified, the 990 became the 990A.

Despite the best efforts of the sales people, only 37 990/990As were completed. Initial operators included Swissair, American Airlines, SAS, Thai International, VARIG, Garuda and APSA Peru. In Europe, the Spanish charter airline Spantax became a major operator of second-hand examples, operating a total of up to 14 over more than ten years; even after the type was replaced, a couple were kept on at Palma, Majorca as stand-by aircraft.

The last Convair 990 flight was in August 1995 when NASA's N810NA completed 20

years of service when it landed back at its base at Edwards, California.

Only a few 990s survive. The best example is Swissair's Coronado HB-ICC at the Swiss Transport Museum at Lucerne. This is maintained in excellent condition complete with its immaculate passenger interior. A couple of old Spantax 990s are possibly still stored at Palma while a maximum of six more still exist in the USA.

Specifications (for a 990A)

Span: 36.58m (120ft 0in)
Length: 42.43m (139ft 5in)
Engines: Four 7,280kg (16,050lb)
    General Electric CJ-805-23B turbofans
Cruise speed: 1,006 km/h (625 mph)
Accommodation: 98 to 121 (Maximum 137)

This Convair 990-30A-6 SE-DAY was one of two leased by SAS from Swissair for a few years in the early 1960s. After service with Swissair and Spantax, it was scrapped at Palma de Mallorca in 1991. (Christian Volpati)

Largest operator of the Coronado outside of the USA was Spantax. Their Coronado EC-BZO is seen here about to depart Gatwick with 149 tourists bound for Palma in February 1984. This aircraft is one of the two that are extant at Palma, Majorca. (Andy Leaver)

A very rare visitor to Gatwick around 1962 was Trans Atlantic Airlines' immaculate C-46A N10435. This aircraft ended her days with Frigorificos Reyes amongst the retired Curtisses at La Paz in Bolivia. (Brian Stainer)

CURTISS C-46 COMMANDO

Curtiss-Wright
St Louis, Missouri
USA

The Curtiss-Wright aircraft company was one of many that attempted to create a competitor for the Douglas DC-3. Their 1936 design, the CW-20 (later known as the C-46 Commando in US military service) was originally envisaged as a 24/34-seat pressurised airliner. The R-2600 Wright Cyclone powered prototype took three years to complete and first flew at St. Louis in March 1940. On the twin-finned prototype, the distinctive fuselage crease of the 'double-bubble' fuselage was originally plated over to give a smooth appearance. However, aerodynamic problems encountered during test flying caused Curtiss-Wright to modify the prototype to CW-20A standard with a large but conventional single fin within a year.

By 1942, when the first production aircraft was finished, the USAAF was badly in need of new large transport aircraft. The Curtiss C-46, with double the cabin volume and 45% increase in gross weight of the DC-3, was therefore ordered in large numbers and extra production lines were set up at Curtiss factories in Buffalo, New York, and Louisville, Kentucky. In total, 3,181 C-46 Commandos were built with the last one delivered in 1945. No civil airliner version was produced until after the war, when surplus aircraft were converted into freighters or passenger transports. In late 1945, Eastern Air Lines ordered the commercial CW-20E transport version, but the availability of cheap ex

military Commandos and Douglas Dakota/Skytrains caused Eastern to cancel. Curtiss never built a civil production CW-20.

Post war, huge numbers of retired USAAF Commandos were bought by airlines in the USA, particularly those operating non-scheduled freight services. Airlines like Riddle, Zantop, Capitol, Slick, Aaxico, and The Flying Tiger Line had large fleets of C-46s in the 1950s and '60s. By the 1980s, the cavernous fuselage and large freight door of the big 'Charlie' was still sought after, particularly in South America. Bolivia, Brazil, Venezuela and Colombia all found the Commando to be ideal for non-scheduled freight services. The Bolivians still operate a handful from La Paz and Cochabamba on mixed freight/passenger services, but since the building of new highways in the country, the famous Bolivian meat haulers are finding it difficult to compete with refrigerated trucks. In 1996 I was honoured to fly in a GPS-equipped C-46 from La Paz, through (not over!) the snow-covered Andes Mountains. The load consisted of 13 passengers (no seats), 11 oil drums and a baby.

All C-46 versions were outwardly similar except for the seventeen C-46E's that had a single cargo door and an old fashioned 'stepped' windshield. In 1952, a C-46F was modified with the addition of two 1.55kN(350lb) thrust 'Palas' turbojets under the wings to boost take-off performance.

Even in 1960, Commandos were still being converted to Super C-46 status, with more powerful engines and increased weights.

The last outposts of C-46 operations are in Alaska, Canada and Bolivia. Fairbanks-based Everts Air Fuel use theirs to move fuel drums and Buffalo Airways, based in the North West Territories, still fly their two immaculate Commandos from Hay River on general cargo duties. Elsewhere, a handful fight over the limited amount of trade in Bolivia alongside stored and dismantled examples hoping for an upturn in business. In California a Commando is flown in USAF colours as a museum exhibit by the Confederate Air Force.

Other stored and preserved examples exist in Brazil, China, Colombia, the Dominican Republic, Japan and Mexico.

Specifications

Span: 32.92m (108ft 0in)
Length: 23.27m (76ft 4in)
Engines: Two 1,495kw (2,000hp) Pratt & Whitney
   R-2800 piston radial engines
Cruise speed: 300km/h (169kts)
Accommodation: Normally 36, maximum 65

Photographed in 1989 over the Caribbean sea by Stephen Piercey, C-46 HI-503CT was once a common sight at Heathrow when it was operated by Lufthansa on European freight services as N9892Z. (Stephen Piercey)

C-46F C-GTPO was bought from Air Manitoba by Buffalo Airways in 1993. This immaculate example of the big 'Charlie' is still in operation at Hay River. Note that Goofy, Donald Duck, Mickey Mouse and Pluto are all passengers! (Henry Tenby)

The first Mercure to be delivered to Air Inter was F-BTTA in June 1974. The aircraft is seen here prior to delivery in November 1973 with the test registration F-WTTA. (Author's collection)

DASSAULT MERCURE

Dassault Aviation
9 Rond-Point Champs Elysées-Marcel Dassault
F-75008, Paris, France

The French Dassault company is world famous for its highly successful series of Mirage jet fighters and in the civilian world, for their long-running series of business jets. The Dassault Mystère 20 (Falcon 20) first introduced in the 1960s has, with nearly 500 built, become their best selling civil aircraft, a claim which can definitely not be made for the Dassault Mercure!

In 1967, Dassault attempted to expand their civil business by investigating designs for a new jet airliner under the designation Mystère 30. With extensive studies revealing a large market for a short-range 150-seater, they commenced detailed design work leading to a final layout that was very similar to the Boeing 737. There were enormous costs involved in launching the new airliner, and so Dassault obtained financial help from the French government with a loan covering 50% of the costs involved in building two prototypes, two static test airframes, aircraft certification and production tooling. A further 30% came from risk-sharing partners, among them Aeritalia of Italy who built the tail-cone and tail unit, CASA of Spain who built the first and second fuselage sections and SABCA of Belgium who built the flaps, spoilers, airbrakes and ailerons. In 1972, Canadair signed an agreement to produce some wing and pylon assemblies in Canada. In anticipation of large airline orders, Dassault built a new factory at Martignas, near

Bordeaux, to manufacture wings for the production Mercures, whilst final assembly of the Mercures took place at another new factory at Istres, near Marseilles.

The first of the two prototypes, fitted with less-powerful JT8D-11 engines, was flown at Bordeaux on 28th May 1971. It carried the contrived registration letters, F-WTCC, the 'TCC' standing for Transport Court-Courier (Short-range transport). The interior diameter was 0.05m (2in) wider than the Boeing 737 although in standard six-abreast layout this was barely noticeable to the passengers.

Despite their intentions to wait until they had received orders for 50 aircraft, Dassault commenced production after just one order for 10 aircraft was received from Air Inter on 29th January 1972. No other orders were received and the whole project became a financial disaster. Even after the Mercure had made its first commercial service in June 1974, the French government continued to subsidise Air Inter because of the high running costs involved with so few aircraft. In 1985, the second prototype was reconfigured to full airline configuration and entered service with Air Inter.

The last Mercure service was on 29th April 1995 between Pau and Paris Orly. Surprisingly for such a small production run, nine of the original twelve still survive. Five are used as instructional airframes at Morlaix, Toulouse, Vitrolles, Bordeaux-Merignac and

at Montpellier where Air Littoral have painted F-BTTE in full Air Littoral colours. Four more are preserved at Paris-Orly, Paris-Le Bourget, Bordeaux-Merignac and one is preserved on poles at the Technic Museum at Speyer in Germany.

Specifications

Span: 30.56m (100ft 3in)
Length: 34.84m (114ft 3½in)
Engines: Two 7030kg (15,00lb)
   Pratt & Whitney JT8D-15 turbofans
Cruise speed: 858km/h (463kts)
Accommodation: 120-150 (maximum 162)

Very rare air-to-air shot of Air Inter Mercure 100 F-BTTG taken in July 1992. Although the type had poor economics, they did give excellent service to Air Inter for 20 years. (Jacques Guillem)

This stunning multicoloured Mercure has been used as a ground instruction airframe by ESMA, the Air Littoral training centre at Montpellier since 1994. (Tony Best)

Seen at Geneva airport in May 1969, Comet 4B G-APMF was later operated by BEA Airtours and Dan-Air London. It was scrapped at Lasham in 1976. (Author's collection)

DE HAVILLAND DH.106 COMET

The de Havilland Aircraft Company Ltd, Hatfield Aerodrome, Herts, and Hawarden Aerodrome Chester, England

In 1944, the British government felt that only a radical new transport aircraft would be able to break the American manufacturers' virtual monopoly on passenger airliners. The Brabazon Committee was therefore formed to encourage manufacturers to submit designs for commercial aircraft for post war service. The de Havilland Aircraft Company proposed their type 106 to meet the Brabazon request for a civilian jet transport.

Discussions with BOAC allowed de Havilland to evolve their initial designs into a 24-seat airliner with a conventional low-wing and four Ghost jet engines buried inside the wings. Prototype construction was commenced amid great secrecy and by 1947, BOAC had showed their confidence in the newly named Comet by ordering 14. With such an advanced aircraft, great attention was paid to static pressure testing of the fuselage, however, these tests were to prove insufficient, and the now infamous Comet accidents in the early 1950s were disastrous for the future British aircraft industry.

First flown at Hatfield on 27th July 1949, the Comet was revealed to the public at the 1949 Farnborough Air Show. Early orders, not all of them to be fulfilled, came from Canadian Pacific, Union Aéromaritime de Transport (UAT), Pan American, LAV Venezuela, Panair do Brasil, Air India, British Commonwealth Pacific Airlines, the Royal Canadian Air Force and Air France.

BOAC flew the world's first jet passenger service with Comet 1 G-ALYP from Heathrow to Johannesburg on 2nd May 1952. However, the high hopes for the airliner were soon shattered by a series of crashes. When two Comets were lost in January and April 1954 in mysterious circumstances, its Certificate of Airworthiness was withdrawn and the whole fleet was grounded. The detailed and lengthy investigation which followed proved that structural failure of the cabin was the cause. Subsequently a few Comet 2s were completed with rounded windows and thicker metal skinning, but the airlines had to wait until the Comet 4 appeared with a redesigned fuselage, increased fuel capacity and more powerful Avon engines, before they could buy Comets with confidence.

Initial airline operators of the Comet 4 and its sub-variants 4B and 4C were BOAC, Aerolineas Argentinas, BEA, Olympic, East African, Mexicana, United Arab, Middle East, Sudan and Kuwait Airways. By acquiring second-hand examples over the course of time, Dan-Air London came to operate the world's largest Comet fleet; altogether 51 Comet 4/4B/4C and ex RAF C.4s were owned, but not necessarily flown, by the Gatwick-based airline. The last civil Comet service was a special Dan-Air commemorative flight in November 1980.

A selection of preserved Comet noses from scrapped examples along with eleven virtually complete Comets in various states of preservation are preserved in the UK. Two are preserved abroad. At Seattle-Paine Field in Washington, the Museum of Flight has restored a Comet 4C for static exhibition in full BOAC colours, (BOAC never had 4C's), and at the incredible Hermeskeil Museum in Germany, a Dan-Air Comet 4 is preserved alongside other British-built classics such as the VC-10, Viscount and Pembroke.

In the UK you can find Comets at Cosford, Duxford, East Fortune, Gatwick, London Colney, Lyneham and Wroughton. The only one currently capable of flight is Comet 4C XS235 'Canopus' at Bruntingthorpe, Leicestershire. This former research aircraft is owned by British Aviation Heritage and is kept in a 'taxiable' condition. Hopefully, problems with the authorities regarding certification will be resolved allowing this historic and significant airliner to fly again.

Specifications (for the Comet 4)

Span: 35.00m (114ft 10in)
Length: 33.99m (111ft 6in)
Engines: Four 5216kg (11,500lb)
  Rolls-Royce Avon 524 turbojets
Cruise speed: 809km/h (503 mph)
Accommodation: 60-76

One of eight Comet 4Cs bought by the Egyptian national airline, United Arab Airlines, SU-AMV was photographed at Heathrow in November 1967. Dan-Air bought this aircraft for spares reclamation in 1976. (Authors Collection)

Currently preserved at Cosford, Comet 1 G-APAS was originally one of three bought by Air France in 1953. Compare the length of its nose to that on the Comet 4 above. (Author)

Series 1 Herons can be identified by their fixed undercarriage. This Heron 1B G-AOXL, originally delivered to Garuda Indonesia, is warming up her Gipsy engines prior to departing with a very light load at Gatwick in February 1969. (Author's collection)

DE HAVILLAND DH.114 HERON

The de Havilland Aircraft Company Ltd
Hatfield Aerodrome, Hertfordshire, and
Hawarden, Chester, England

Details of a larger, four-engined, 'feeder liner' based around the successful de Havilland Dove were revealed in 1949. To expedite construction, as well as to provide some commonality of type for the operators, the Heron prototype was built at Hatfield using many Dove components including the nose, tail and outer wings. This Series 1 aircraft had a fixed undercarriage with a castoring nose wheel and was powered by four 185kW (250hp) Gipsy Queen 30 six-cylinder air-cooled piston engines. I don't know if passengers were considered to be more athletic in those days, but the positioning of the three emergency exits in the roof would today seem a bit unhelpful in an evacuation.

The Heron 1 was granted its Certificate of Airworthiness in November 1950. Altogether, 52 Series 1 Herons were built at Hatfield (7) and Chester (45). Early operators of the Series 1 included BEA, Braathens, Garuda, Japan Air Lines, Jersey Airlines, New Zealand National Airways, PLUNA and UTA.

The prototype of the faster and more economical Series 2 with retractable undercarriage was completed and flown in December 1952 at Hatfield prior to all production switching to Chester around 1953. These sturdy and reliable transports were ideal for feeder services and for operations from short or unprepared runways. They also became popular as executive transports with companies such as Shell, Ferranti, Rolls-

Royce, Philips, Fiat, Vickers-Armstrong and English Electric. Probably the most famous Herons were the four aircraft (one Mk.2B, two 2Ds and one Mk.4) operated by the Queen's Flight at Benson from 1955 for more than ten years. Other VIP Herons were 'owned' by King Hussein, King Feisal II, President Nkrumah, Prince Talal al Saud, the Sultan of Morocco and the Belgian Royal family.

To improve the payload and speed of the Gipsy-powered Herons, several examples were re-engineered to accept Lycoming engines. Between 1966 and 1974, the Riley Aeronautics Corporation of Florida converted about 20 Series 2 Herons to 'Riley Turbo Skyliners' with four turbo-supercharged 290 hp Lycoming IO-540 engines and Hartzell three-blade props. Eight further Riley Herons were completed by Connellan Airways of Alice Springs in Australia, and Prinair of Puerto Rico (a famously prolific Heron operator) converted 29. In Japan, six Series 1 Herons of Toa Airways were converted to Lycoming power by Shin Meiwa. The most radical Heron conversion was the twin-engined Saunders ST-27 (see page 130).

About half-a-dozen Herons are still airworthy. In Australia, Heron Airlines at Sydney-Bankstown use one Riley and one Gipsy powered example in 15-seat configuration for local charter flights. In Jersey, the 'Friends of the Heron' preservation group commendably keep one flying in full

Jersey Airlines colours. In the UK, one is preserved outside the defunct Croydon Airport in the colour scheme of the last aircraft to fly from there, one other is preserved at the Newark Air Museum in Nottinghamshire, and another is at the de Havilland Aircraft Heritage Centre (formerly Mosquito Aircraft Museum) at London Colney in Hertfordshire. A few others survive in the USA, Malaysia, New Zealand, Norway and Sri Lanka.

Specifications

Span: 21.80m (71ft 6in)
Length: 14.80m (48ft 6in)
Engines: Four 185kW (250hp)
Gipsy Queen 30 piston engines
Cruise speed: 307km/h (166kts)
Accommodation: 14

Originally delivered to Cambrian Airways as G-AOGO in 1956, Heron 2 N585PR was converted to Lycoming power in 1978 for service with the world's largest Heron operator, San Juan-based Prinair. (Bernard King)

The opportunity to fly in a Heron is still a reality. The immaculate Jersey-based G-AORG, preserved in original Jersey Airlines colours, often visits European airshows to fly in the display and to provide joy rides where permitted. (Frank McMeiken)

Guyana Airways operated two DHC-4A Caribou alongside a couple of Twin Otters and a DC-6 when this rare passenger-carrying example was photographed in 1972. (Author's collection)

DE HAVILLAND CANADA DHC-4 CARIBOU
de Havilland Canada
Downsview, Ontario
Canada

The Caribou was the result of discussions between de Havilland Canada and the US and Canadian armies in 1956. Both armies required a twin-engined tactical support airlifter that had the load capacity of the Douglas C-47 and the STOL capabilities of the DHC Otter. Assisted by the Canadian Department of Defence, DHC built a prototype which incorporated many useful design features including the highly practical rear fuselage ramp which allowed direct loading of vehicles and artillery. It could also be opened in flight for parachuting men and equipment. The huge high-mounted 'gull' wings kept propeller blades clear of any debris, especially when operating from unprepared strips and the cabin could accommodate 32 fully equipped troops or 24 paratroopers. In the CASEVAC layout the Caribou could carry 14 stretchers plus 12 sitting casualties or medics.

The prototype first flew at Downsview on 30th July 1958 and the US Army received five pre-production examples for evaluation as the YAC-1 in 1959. The type was considered excellent for US Army service and was officially accepted after the US Secretary of Defense waived the 2,268kg (5,000lb) upper weight limit for army fixed-wing aircraft. The Royal Canadian Air Force initially ordered two Caribous as the CC-108.

A four-month worldwide sales tour by the DHC demonstrator aircraft in late 1959 visited 47 countries and attracted military sales from Australia, Ghana, India, Kenya and Kuwait. Initially, the Caribou's civil use was limited; however civil sales were made to Ansett-MAL in New Guinea, AMOCO in Ecuador, and CAT in Taiwan. Later civil operations were in Canada, Costa Rica, Gabon and South Africa. The most famous 'civil' operator of the type was Air America, whose clandestine operations in Laos were highlighted in the Hollywood movie of the same name.

Of the 307 Caribous built, the US Army and Air Force operated 159 as the AC-1, CV-2A, CV-2B, C-7A and C-7B. US and Australian Air Force Caribous were extensively used in the Viet Nam war and captured US Caribous were operated by the North Vietnamese Air Force until the late 1970s.

After the first 24 had been completed, the maximum take-off weight was increased, creating the DHC-4A which remained in production until 1973. In the 1990s, NewCal Aviation of New Jersey saw a potential market for a turboprop-powered Caribou. They bought up large numbers of retired military aircraft and converted one with 1,062kW (1,424shp) PT6A –67R engines and four-bladed props. This DHC-4T first flew in November 1991 but later crashed.

The type has proved useful in specialist configurations. In 1960, DHC used a Caribou to test the General Electric YT-64-GE4 gas turbine engines for their DHC-5 Buffalo and in recent years the Environmental Research Institute of Michigan, 'ERIM', have used a Caribou for scientific research flights. Apart from converting several ex-military aircraft to civil freighters, NewCal Aviation's workshop in Malta converted one for 'Advanced Maritime Pollution Control'.

Currently, the Australian Air Force still operates about a dozen, and their replacement should be announced soon. Worldwide civil operations have all but disappeared; however Greatland Air Cargo is believed to fly a couple at Anchorage, Alaska, Vintage Props and Jets have one in Florida and Interocean Airways at Brakpan in South Africa still have four Caribous in their fleet. At least 15 US military Caribous are preserved in the USA and others are preserved in Spain and Malaysia. No civil Caribous are preserved; however dozens of civilian survivors are stored in America, particularly with Pen Turbo Aviation who have 33 Caribous including a turboprop conversion at Cape May County Airport in New Jersey. Others are believed to exist in Beira (Mozambique), Ecuador and Malta.

Specifications (for the DHC-4A)

Span: 29.15m (95ft 7⅛in)
Length: 22.13m (72ft 7in)
Engines: Two 1,082kW (1,450shp)
  Pratt & Whitney R-2000-7M2 piston radials
Cruise speed: 293km/h (158kts)
Accommodation: 30 passengers
Payload: 3,965kg (8,620lb)

The smart red and black colour scheme on this radar equipped Caribou emphasises the pronounced droop on the Pratt & Whitney R-2000 engines. Registered in Mozambique, Interocean's Caribou C9-ATV was photographed at Jan Smuts airport in South Africa in 1990. (Author's collection)

Previously operated in Canada by Air Tindi, N112CH is currently flown by Vintage Props and Jets from its base at New Smyrna Beach in Florida. (Author's collection)

Until recently, DC-2 NC1934D was kept in beautiful airworthy condition by a group of Douglas employees at Long Beach in California. The aircraft is still at Long Beach, but its condition is not as nice as it was here in 1986. (EMCS)

DOUGLAS DC-2

Douglas Aircraft Company
Santa Monica, California
USA

Around 1930, American domestic airline services were flown with a variety of small airliners built by makers such as Curtiss, Fokker, Boeing and Stinson. Most of these were built with wooden spars and they were slow and uncomfortable. One successful attempt at an all-metal airliner was built by Ford. Their remarkable Tri-Motor set the standard for air travel in the late 1920s, but public demand for faster and more comfortable aircraft together with the Bureau of Air Commerce's demand for inspections of wooden-winged airliners forced the manufacturers to try new and advanced materials and produce a better aircraft.

Boeing offered the excellent Model 247, but United's order for 60 aircraft was to tie up the production line for two years. Other airlines were thus forced to try other manufacturers for their new airliners. In August 1932, the vice president of Transcontinental and Western Air (the precursor of the current TWA) wrote to five US aircraft manufacturers announcing their interest in acquiring ten or more 12-seater tri-motor monoplanes to be used as sleeper transports. TWA's toughest requirement was that the new aircraft should be able to take off from any TWA-used airport with a full load and one engine inoperative. Using advanced wing, fuselage, flap and cowling designs based on the Northrop Alpha, the Douglas Aircraft Company was able to design and build the one and only twin-

engined 12-passenger DC-1 (Douglas Commercial-1) in 1933. Both the new Wright Cyclone and Pratt & Whitney Hornet radial piston engines were offered to power this remarkable airliner and after extensive testing, TWA were happy with the twin-engined layout and ordered 20 production models, to be known as the DC-2. These were slightly longer than the DC-1 and had more powerful engines with controllable pitch propellers and 14 seats.

The first DC-2 flew on 11th May 1934 and entered TWA service a week later. Other US airlines to order the DC-2 included American, Braniff, Eastern, Pan American and PANAGRA. Overseas buyers included ALI (Italy), CLS (Czechoslovakia), Holyman's (Australia), KLM, KNILM (Netherlands East Indies) LAPE (Spain), LOT and Swissair. In 1934, a KLM DC-2 won the transport category in the MacRobertson London-Australia Air Race. The only aircraft to complete the course in a faster time was the specially built DH.88 Comet racer G-ACSS.

Douglas built 193 DC-2s (130 for civil use), proving the basic layout and providing Douglas with its first commercial success. Licences to build the type were sold to Fokker in Holland and Nakajima Hikoki Kabushinki Kaisha in Japan. Although Fokker never actually built any, they did assemble and sell 39 DC-2s using Douglas-built components. The Japanese built five DC-2s for Greater

Japan Air Lines. The last DC-2 was delivered in July 1937 and over the next ten years most were replaced by DC-3s.

About nine DC-2s survive worldwide. In the USA you can find preserved DC-2s at the USAF museum at Wright-Patterson AFB (USAAF C-39A) and at Long Beach in California (Douglas Historical Foundation). Three are preserved in Australia, two are in Finland and the famous air race aircraft, PH-AJU, is stored dismantled at Amsterdam airport. In November 1999, it was announced that the Dutch National Aviation Museum had, thanks to a generous donation from KLM, raised enough funds to buy the airworthy DC-2 which had been owned since 1968 by Mr Colgate Darden III of Edmund, South Carolina. This aircraft, painted to represent PH-AJU, was flown via the UK to Holland in August 1999 to promote interest and help raise funds for the purchase.

Specifications

Span: 25.91m (85ft 0in)
Length: 18.89m (61ft 11½in)
Engines: Two 535kW (720hp)
 Pratt & Whitney R-1690 Hornet, or 559kW
 (750hp) Bristol Pegasus VI, or 652kW (875hp)
 Wright Cyclone SGR 1820 piston radials
Cruise speed: 318km/h (198mph)
Accommodation: 14

The real PH-AJU is currently dismantled and stored in a hangar at Amsterdam Schiphol airport. However, this old Australian Air Force DC-2 is preserved at Albury in New South Wales to represent the record-breaking aircraft. (Mike Green)

The world's last airworthy DC-2, NC39165, has been owned by Colgate Darden III of Edmund, South Carolina since 1968. In August 1999, it flew the Atlantic to Bruntingthorpe in the UK where it was photographed prior to departing to its new home in Holland. (Steve Kinder)

This Douglas DC-3, CF-TDS, served with TCA from July 1946 until October 1956 when it was sold to Quebecair. Less than 2 years later it was destroyed by fire in the Province of Quebec. (Air Canada Archives)

DOUGLAS DC-3 & C-47

Douglas Aircraft Company
Santa Monica, California
USA

Some readers may question my choice of 'Classic' airliners; however, I guarantee that none would argue that the immortal DC-3/C-47 does not deserve a place in this book. The Dakota is the all-time Classic airliner.

The DC-3 evolved from the DC-1 and DC-2 and started out as a sleeper transport designed specifically at the request of C R Smith of American Airlines in 1934. He required an aircraft that had the economics and performance of the DC-2 and the interior spaciousness of their Curtiss Condor IIs. The DST (Douglas Sleeper Transport) was based on the DC-2 but had a wider fuselage, longer wings, a larger fin and more powerful engines. First flown on 17th December 1935, the DST had sleeping berths for 14 and could be identified by the small windows over the bunks in the upper fuselage. Only forty DST were built, but it was the 21-seat 'day plane' DC-3 that captured all the orders and became a best seller with the world's airlines. Prior to the USA joining in the Second World War, Douglas sold 417 for airline use, but it was the wartime American military requirement for a large fleet of transport aircraft that saw the production lines turning out huge quantities of C-47s. A large number of variants under a multitude of designations were completed for the Army, Navy, Air Force and Marines.

Ten thousand military versions of the DC-3, known as the C-47 Skytrain in America, and the Dakota in Britain, were built by Douglas in Santa Monica, Long Beach and Oklahoma City. In addition, other US aeronautical companies completed more than 2,500. In February 1938, the American-based Mitsui and Company Ltd, a subsidiary of the Mitsui Trading Company of Japan, obtained a licence to build and sell the DC-3 in Japan and Manchukuo. They subcontracted production to Nakajima and Showa who built nearly 500 DC-3s in nine different versions under the designation L2D. Known by the Allies as the 'Tabby', the L2D was the Japanese Navy's standard military transport aircraft during the war. A similar arrangement was made with manufacturing rights in the Soviet Union around 1940. The USSR initially obtained 22 DC-3s and used some of these as patterns to build the Shvetsov M-62-powered PS-84. The type was later designated Lisunov Li-2 and powered by the Ash-62 engine. Altogether 6,127 were built initially at Chimki in Moscow, but following the German advance the production line was moved to Tashkent.

Post-war, hundreds of C-47s were snapped up at bargain prices by the world's airlines and converted for civilian use. Many of today's great airlines were started with a small fleet of DC-3s. These include Aloha Airlines, Aviateca, Cathay Pacific, Copa Panama, Cyprus Airways, Ethiopian Airlines, Garuda, Indian Airlines, JAT, Kuwait Airways, Ladeco, Martinair, Philippine Airlines, Saudi Arabian Airlines, TAP, Transbrasil, Tunisair and Turkish Airlines.

Current duties for remaining DC-3/C-47s include non-scheduled passenger and freight, skydiver transport, anti-mosquito spraying, rain cloud seeding, pollution control, aerial surveying, enthusiast and nostalgia trips and humanitarian relief work. Despite their use by virtually every air force in the world, very few military examples are currently in service, but turboprop-powered DC-3 conversions have proved quite popular with air forces in Central America and South Africa.

By far the largest number of survivors are in the USA. Others are in Central America and Australia, while in Europe, the largest fleet of operational DC-3s is owned by Coventry-based Air Atlantique. There are probably no more than 150 DC-3/C-47s in flying condition worldwide but there are hundreds more stored, dumped or preserved, making the total number around 1000. No Japanese-built L2Ds are believed to survive, but more than 30 examples of the Li-2 reportedly still exist intact in the FSU, Hungary, China, Romania and Poland. A single Russian Li-2 is currently preserved in flying condition near Moscow.

Specifications (for the C-47A)

Span: 29.11m (95ft 6in)
Length: 19.43m (63ft 9in)
Engines: Two 895kW (1,200hp) Pratt & Whitney Twin Wasp R-1830 piston radial engines
Cruise speed: 266km/h (143kts)
Accommodation: 32 maximum

A rare air-to-air photographic sortie by the author was in 1982 when I accompanied Steve Piercey in a Piper Seneca to capture this shot of Air Atlantique DC-3 G-AMPO, still in basic Eastern Airways colours, flying out of Staverton. (Author)

In recent years, the preservation of airliner types in South Africa has been very strong. Thanks to South African Airways, a fleet of immaculate DC-3s, DC-4s and a Ju-52 are available for air show appearances and passenger charters. (Richard Ness)

Seen at Tucson in January 1994, this Super DC-3 (C-117) displays the registration and original colour scheme that was carried by the prototype Super DC-3 in 1949. Note the square shaped wingtips and tail. (Author)

DOUGLAS SUPER DC-3 (DC-3S)

Douglas Aircraft Company
Santa Monica, California
USA

Prompted by the major US airlines, the Civil Aeronautics Authority threatened new Civil Air Regulations in the late 1940s which would ground hundreds of the war surplus aircraft in use as airliners and freighters with the US non-scheduled carriers. If these rules, planned for introduction in 1952, came into force, Douglas knew that there would be a ready market for a commercial transport to replace their DC-3s and C-47s. Sensing a new business opportunity, Douglas committed design staff to work on the new model, but rather than waste time and money on designing and building a totally new aeroplane, Douglas judged that a modernised DC-3 could do the job just as well. They bought two second-hand aircraft to use as prototypes and stripped them down prior to commencing work on the DC-3S, better known as the Super DC-3.

The most important tasks were to rectify the DC-3's poor take-off performance and unsatisfactory operation on one engine. Douglas also knew that a significant improvement in cruising speed would help sales. The easiest way of achieving these goals was to fit more powerful engines. The Super DC-3 was therefore offered with either the 1,475 hp Wright Cyclone or the 1,450 hp P&W R-2000. Structural changes included a strengthened fuselage with a 0.99m (3ft 3in) 'plug' forward of the main spar, new aerodynamically-improved engine cowlings

and undercarriage fairings and a larger area, square-tipped fin and tailplane. The already strong wing centre section was left alone, but the all-new shorter-span outer wings had squared tips and a 15.5° sweep on the leading edge and a 4° sweep on the trailing edge. The undercarriage was strengthened to cope with the higher weights and a partially retractable tailwheel was provided. The extended cabin could seat 30 and boarding was made easier with an integral air stair in the passenger door.

The Super DC-3 first flew at Clover Field on 23rd June 1949 and initial trials revealed a performance better than expected including a 20% increase in cruising speed compared to the DC-3C. The second aircraft was completed while the first commenced a 10,000-mile sales tour of the USA, Canada and Mexico. However, by this time the purpose-built modern 'DC-3 replacements', the Martin 2-0-2/4-0-4 and the Convair 240/340 were appearing, some with pressurisation, and the CAA had backed down with their proposal to ground the older DC-3s. The only airline order for the Super DC-3 came from Capital Airlines in 1949. They sold three of their DC-3s to Douglas and in 1950 bought them back for $275,000 each as Cyclone–powered Super DC-3s.

With much invested in the research and development of the Super DC-3, Douglas were anxious to find customers. Hoping for an order, Douglas sold the prototype to the USAF

but they rejected it and gave it to the Navy in 1951. The USN, unlike the USAF, was so impressed that they ordered 100 conversions to be made from a selection of their R4Ds. The aircraft, initially known as the R4D-8 and after 1962 the C-117, survived US Naval and Marines service until retirement in 1976.

As usual with many well maintained ex US military transport types, there was a market for them among the civil freight haulers particularly in Canada and the USA. By the late 1980s cargo airlines operating C-117 Super DC-3s included SkyFreighters in Texas and Air Dale, Air 500 and Millardair in Canada.

Currently, one C-117 is preserved in Iceland and at least three are preserved in the USA at Pensacola, Tucson and El Toro. About 20 are still stored in yards around the AMARC at Davis-Monthan in Arizona in addition to about 15 to 20 civil examples stored elsewhere in America. Since the demise of Mabuhay Airways' C-117 near Manila in August 1999, the only operational examples outside the USA appear to be in Canada. Gateway Airlines in Ontario have three and Kenn Borek Air has one at Calgary in Alberta.

Specifications

Span: 27.43m (90ft)
Length: 20.75m (67ft 9in)
Engines: Two 1,100kW (1,475hp)
    Wright Cyclone R-1820 piston radials
Cruise speed: 400km/h (251 mph)
Accommodation: 30

C-117D RP-C473 was photographed in storage at Manila in March 1995. In December that year the aircraft was sold to local airline Mabuhay Airways and repainted in a white colour scheme. She was written off in a forced landing near Manila on 30th August 1999. (Author)

One of the few current commercial operators of the Super DC-3 is Kenn Borek Air of Calgary, Alberta. C-GGKG displays its high visibility markings at its base in 1995. (Author's collection)

Coventry-based Ace Freighters bought this 1946-vintage DC-4-1009 in 1964. It is seen parked on the famous Heathrow south ramp in October that year. Two years later she was retired to her base where she was later scrapped. (Authors collection)

DOUGLAS DC-4

Douglas Aircraft Company
Santa Monica, California
USA

In 1935, Douglas responded to a request from United Air Lines for a four-engined long-range airliner. Despite reservations about the expense of designing and building a new large airliner, Douglas committed itself to initial design studies and after the five major US airlines all gave $100,000 to Douglas to help with prototype costs, they built a large triple-finned airliner that was given the sequential designation DC-4. The aircraft was flown in trials by United Air Lines but it proved to be too complex and expensive to operate. Only one of this DC-4 variant was built. The subsequent design and production of the simplified C-54/DC-4 series made Douglas re-designate the original three-finned aircraft as the DC-4E ('E' for experimental).

The airlines' need for a large airliner still remained so Douglas re-thought their design and offered a new DC-4 that was lighter and less complex in its construction. Great attention was paid to the provision of better economics, simple construction and ease of maintenance. The new DC-4 was much smaller than the DC-4E with a circular cross-section fuselage, single fin and a tricycle undercarriage based on the DC-4E's.

With the war raging and US government demands for more military aircraft restricting Douglas's efforts to produce a civil airliner, the company completed the first DC-4 and flew it in military markings from Clover Field in Santa Monica on 14th February 1942. When

America entered the Second World War, all DC-4 production was requisitioned by the US military and the type was given the designation C-54 Skymaster.

More than 1,200 C-54s of various marks were supplied to the USAAF. After the war, the hundreds of surviving surplus military transport aircraft, including C-54s, were made available for sale to the world's airlines. This proved to be a problem for Douglas, who could not find buyers for its new and improved DC-4-1009 aircraft. Only 78 of this unpressurised 44-seater transport were built post-war for civil orders.

In 1945 the Canadair company, based at Cartierville, Canada, commenced production of the DC-4 under license from Douglas. Seventy of these Rolls-Royce Merlin powered versions were built as the Canadair C-4 North Star. (See page 54). Twenty-one DC-4/C-54s were converted by Aviation Traders to ATL 98 Carvair configuration in the 1960s. These aircraft are described on page 28.

Thanks to its ruggedness and simplicity, the DC-4/C-54 survived in worldwide use for many years. Several Skymasters are still flying today, mostly as freighters; however Buffalo Airways and Air North of Canada, still operate DC-4s equipped to carry true fare-paying passengers. Elsewhere, some recently retired South African Air Force examples have been bought by preservation groups both in South Africa and Holland. The SAA Historic

Flight, now moved to Swartkop, is responsible for two immaculate passenger DC-4s which provide enthusiast and tourist flights to piston fans in South Africa. These aircraft have even been to the USA and Europe in recent years allowing many people the opportunity to ride in one of these beautifully restored airliners. The Dutch Dakota Association similarly operates a single DC-4 in Holland. A handful of DC-4s still operate in the USA as water-bombers. These aircraft have all unnecessary weight removed from their fuselages and have huge tanks fitted either in, or under, the fuselage to carry the fire retardant liquid. These aircraft often spend many months on the ground awaiting 'call-up' to a forest fire anywhere on the US mainland.

Preserved military C-54s can be found in Colombia, Germany, Hawaii, Korea, Saudi Arabia, Spain, Taiwan, Turkey and the USA. Civil survivors exist in Australia, Belgium, Bolivia, Canada, Colombia, Holland, the Philippines, South Africa, the USA and the Democratic Republic of Congo.

Specifications

Span: 35.81m (117ft 6in)
Length: 28.60m (93ft 10in)
Engines: Four 1,080kW (1,450shp)
    Pratt & Whitney R-2000-2SD-BG
    Twin Wasp radial piston engines
Cruise speed: 365km/h (197kts)
Accommodation: 86 maximum
Freighter payload: 14,742kg (32,500lb)

This ex-United States Air Force C-54D C9-ATS was bought by Mozambique airline Interocean Airways in 1991 and photographed in 1997. Other previous operators of this aircraft include the Royal Danish Air Force and Millardair in Canada. (Martin Siegrist).

This colourful and immaculately finished C-54E C-GCTF is operated as a Tanker/Freighter by NWT-based Buffalo Airways amongst a mixed fleet of vintage C-46s, DC-3s and Catalinas. (AviationTrade Switzerland)

DC-6B N93117 was newly delivered to Western Air Lines on 9th October 1956. After service with Japan Air Lines, Fratflug Iceland, Pomair and Iscargo it was withdrawn from use in Iceland in 1977. (Erik Bernhard collection)

DOUGLAS DC-6

Douglas Aircraft Company
Santa Monica, California
USA

This truly classic airliner was originally conceived as a stretched and pressurised upgrade of the high-selling DC-4/C-54 (see page 82). The DC-6 was sold to airlines all over the world, and its reliability, adaptability and low operating costs mean that, 54 years after its first flight, there are still a handful of DC-6s gainfully employed around the world, while its original rival, the Lockheed Constellation, is relegated to museums and preservation groups.

The DC-6 uses the same wing as the DC-4, but with more powerful engines and a DC-4 fuselage stretched by 2.06m (81in) and converted to allow for pressurisation. The old fashioned oval windows of the DC-4 were also replaced by 'modern' rectangular items. This modification caused some DC-4 operators to paint rectangular black edges to their round windows to give the impression to their passengers that they were boarding the more modern DC-6. Once inside, this illusion was obviously lost! The Six's three cockpit-crew were provided with latest radio and navigation equipment, and all the airframe leading edges were provided with a highly efficient de-icing system to cope with the higher cruising altitudes.

More than a year before the first flight of the prototype DC-6 (XC-112A) from Santa Monica in February 1946, American Airlines ordered 50 DC-6s in order to compete with TWA's fleet of sleek Lockheed Constellations

on US transcontinental services. Other US operators to order the new DC-6 included Braniff, Delta, National, Panagra and United Air Lines.

175 of the original 'straight' DC-6 version were built. These were followed by 74 of the stretched 1.52m (5ft 0in) DC-6A 'Liftmaster'. This version, first flown in September 1949, was initially built without cabin windows as a pure freighter. It had a reinforced floor, two upward opening main-deck cargo doors and new, more powerful, Double Wasp engines with water/methanol injection and different propellers. Some DC-6As were later converted to passenger use while others were built as convertible passenger/freight DC-6Cs, an early example of the popular 'Quick Change' format.

Built alongside the DC-6A and C was the best-selling DC-6B. First flown on 2nd February 1951, 288 of this pure passenger airliner were built at Santa Monica before production stopped. The 6Bs were similar to the 6As but they were built without the freight doors and strengthened floor. Largest operator of the DC-6 series, with 168 aircraft, was the US Military (Air Force/Navy/Marines). Their DC-6s were given the designations C-118 or R6D.

Various unofficial designations (DC-6AB, DC-6AC, DC-6A[C], DC-6BF) were applied to the DC-6s modified to freighters after withdrawal from front-line service. The unique

pair of DC-6Bs that were converted to swing-tail freighter configuration by Sabena in Belgium are still in service with Alaska-based Northern Air Cargo who currently operate the world's largest fleet of 13 DC-6s.

In all, 704 'Sixes' were built, the last two were delivered to Jugoslovenski Aerotransport (JAT) late in 1958. Both of these have been restored to luxurious 66-seat passenger configuration and until recently, one was flying tourist services in Namibia for Namibia Commercial Aviation. Other airworthy DC-6s can be found freighting in Colombia, England and the USA; however a few are still serving as fire-bombers in America having been converted to carry up to 3,000 US gallons (11,356 litres) of liquid fire retardant. Some Sixes are used to carry fuel in special tanks to remote communities, especially in Alaska.

Preserved/stored/dumped examples can be found in Bolivia, Brazil, Denmark, Domini-can Republic, Ecuador, Egypt, Ethiopia, France, Haiti, Italy, Mexico, Paraguay, Peru, Portugal, Switzerland, Syria, Taiwan, USA and the Democratic Republic of Congo.

Specifications (for the DC-6B)

Span: 35.81m (117ft 6in)
Length: 32.18m (105ft 7in)
Engines: Four 1,685kW (2,500hp) Pratt & Whitney R-2800 Double Wasp radial pistons
Cruise speed: 501km/h (270kts)
Accommodation: 102 maximum
Payload: 12,786kg (28,188lb)

Stephen Piercey took this evocative photo of DC-6BF CP-1650 loading up at Rurrenabaque in Bolivia in May 1984. Note the treacherous mountain scenery and the lack of ground equipment at this grass strip. (Stephen Piercey)

Until 1999, this Namibian registered DC-6B was flown on special tourist flights from its base at Windhoek. Namibia Commercial Aviation flew it in a luxury 66-seat layout under the title 'Classic Air Travel'. (Author's collection)

This March 1966 colour slide depicts one of Conair's five magnificent DC-7s at Copenhagen Airport. Previously operated by American Airlines, ONA, Pacific Western and Flying Enterprise, OY-DMU was scrapped in 1969. (Author's collection)

DOUGLAS DC-7

Douglas Aircraft Company
Santa Monica, California
USA

Douglas first used the DC-7 designation on a proposed post-war civil transport version of the C-74 Globemaster 1 which was offered to Pan American. This project was dropped, allowing the unused DC-7 designation to reappear in 1951 on a new design. The DC-7 was, in essence, a larger and more powerful version of the DC-6 that became Douglas's last piston-engined transport.

Douglas were initially concerned that work on a new design would siphon profits from their highly successful DC-6 line; however, when American Airlines ordered 25 aircraft straight from the drawing board, Douglas began production. Not surprisingly, much of the design of the DC-7 was a carry over from the earlier DC-4/DC-6 but with the addition of the new and more powerful 'Turbo-Compound' engines which used the engine exhaust to drive a turbine coupled to the crankshaft. The Seven's wing, (the same span as the DC-6) was strengthened to support the new engines but it was still based on the much smaller C-54/DC4. The new fuselage was basically that of the DC-6B but with a 1.02m (3ft 4in) stretch. The Wright R-3350 eighteen-cylinder radial engines needed massive four-bladed constant speed propellers and the 'new' design had a stronger undercarriage that could be lowered at high speed for use as air brakes.

The prototype DC-7 first flew in May 1953, and in October, the first of an order for 34 was delivered to American Airlines. All of the 105 DC-7s were sold to US trunk carriers; United had 57, Delta 10 and National 4.

The improved DC-7B (there was no DC-7A) was first flown in October 1954. This had uprated 18DA-4 engines, but apart from the extended engine nacelles which could be fitted with extra fuel tanks, it was externally identical to the early version. These tanks were deleted from the aircraft operated on US domestic services, but Pan American and South African Airways both needed the extra fuel capacity for their long-range schedules. Pan Am commenced non-stop DC-7B services from New York to London in June 1955.

Because of the prevailing westerly winds, Pan Am's DC-7Bs often had to make a refuelling stop in Greenland on the return trip to the USA. This embarrassing delay was thankfully eliminated when Pan Am prompted Douglas to build a DC-7B with even more fuel capacity. The resulting aircraft became the world's first truly long-distance civil transport, the magnificent DC-7C. First flown in December 1955, and later given the appropriate name 'Seven Seas', the DC-7C gained its extra range by extending each inner wing by 1.02m (5ft) inboard of the engines. This space was used for additional fuel but it also moved the engines further from the cabin, reducing noise and vibration for the passengers. A further stretch to the fuselage of 1.10m (3ft 6in) brought the passenger capacity to 105.

Very soon, the reign of the piston-powered airliners as front line equipment for the major airlines collapsed. With the appearance of the Comet, Boeing 707 and DC-8, the world's airlines started buying jets. Their DC-7s were gradually relegated to the less prestigious passenger routes or modified for freight work with the 'unofficial' designations DC-7F/7BF/7CF and 7(C)F. In the late sixties/early seventies, the DC-7 became popular with the various US based travel clubs which operated outside the normal airline regulations. Other DC-7s were modified for use as water bombers and one aircraft was even used as a pylon racer in the USA!

Most of the surviving DC-7s are in the USA. Currently, Europe has a couple of airworthy Sevens based at Cordoba in Spain for fire bombing, while the airports at Geneva and Copenhagen have one each for fire service use. One is used as an advertising hoarding at Las Palmas and the Musée de L'Air has a former French military example at Le Bourget.

Specifications (for the DC-7C)

Span: 38.86m (127ft 6in)
Length: 34.21m (112ft 3in)
Engines: Four 2,535kW (3,400hp) Wright R-3350-18EA-1 Turbo-Compound radial piston engines
Cruise speed: 571km/h (425kts)
Accommodation: 105

One of my favourite shots shows Saturn Airways DC-7C N90773 at Manchester Airport in September 1967. This aircraft was originally delivered to BOAC at Heathrow as G-AOIG in 1956. (Author's collection)

Active DC-7s are now a very rare sight. This firebombing DC-7 'Tanker 66' N6353C belongs to Butler Aircraft and was brilliantly captured by Martyn Cooper at Coeur d'Alene in September 1998. (Martyn Cooper)

This 1960-vintage DC-8-31 had already flown for Pan American-Grace (Panagra) and Braniff Airways before Capitol purchased it in 1967 and made it one of their 'CapitoLiners'. (Author's collection)

DOUGLAS DC-8-10/20/30/40/50

Douglas Aircraft Company
3855 Lakewood Boulevard, Long Beach
California 90846, USA

The birth of Douglas's first commercial jetliner was spoilt by the US government's decision to order the Boeing KC-135, a military tanker equivalent of the Boeing 707. This affected the sales prospects for the DC-8, and caused Douglas to suffer financially for many years. Gone were the days of Douglas being the world's leading manufacturer of commercial airliners; Boeing was now the new king.

Despite the setback Douglas announced in June 1955 that production of their DC-8 would go ahead using private finance. In September, Pan American ordered 25 DC-8 Series 30s, and by the year end Douglas had orders for 98 aircraft from seven airlines. With a fuselage designed for six-across seating (the 707 had five-across), construction of the first DC-8 commenced at Long Beach in February 1957. A prototype was not built, partly because a full-scale mock-up, costing $7.5 million, had provided Douglas with much of the constructional information required. First flight was in May 1958 and first airline deliveries were to Delta and United,

Standard length DC-8s were produced in five series sub-divided into 16 models, but initially Douglas offered three types to the airlines. The Series 10, with JT3 engines, was designed for domestic services. The Series 20, with more powerful JT4A engines, was intended for services to 'hot-and-high' airports, and the Series 30 also with JT4A engines but with greater fuel capacity, was

offered for intercontinental services.

The first order for the 'Intercontinental' series 30 was for 25 aircraft for Pan American in September 1955. This was followed by further orders from Eastern, KLM, JAL, National, SAS and United.

In May 1956, Trans-Canada Air Lines launched the Series 40 with an order for four aircraft. This series was similar to the 30 but had Rolls-Royce Conway engines. Other operators who ordered the Conway-powered DC-8-40 were Alitalia and Canadian Pacific. None of these are currently flying.

When Pratt & Whitney produced the JT3D-1 turbofan engine, Douglas were able to offer the new Series 50 in 1960. No other changes to the DC-8 were required other than a re-design of the engine pylons and nacelles. The fan-powered Series 50 was a great improvement over previous models. It was quieter; it had greater range and was more economic. In April 1961 the convertible Series 50CF was announced. This had a strengthened floor with associated cargo handling systems and a large forward cargo door. Given the name 'Jet Trader', the 39 original build Series 50CFs were later joined by examples which had been converted from earlier Series 30, 40 and 50s by Douglas at Tulsa. Fifteen examples of an all-freight DC-8 Series 50AF with virtually no fuselage windows and all passenger equipment deleted were built for United Airlines.

The Burbank Aeronautical Corp and Quiet Nacelle Corp have both developed Stage 3 hushkits for the Series 50. This will allow many of the short-fuselage survivors (all of them are Series 50 freighters) to continue to operate in Europe and North America. One of the largest fleets of Stage II compliant DC-8 Series 50s is operated by Miami-based Fine Air who also have a Series 50 flying with Stage 3 hushkitted engines. Countries without strict noise controls such as Swaziland, Liberia, Ghana and Colombia still rely on their non-hushed DC-8-50s for cargo operations.

Airworthy short-bodied DC-8s can still be found particularly in the USA and Central and South America. Surprisingly, the first DC-8 (N8008D) is still in existence at Marana, Arizona, and other examples are preserved in China, Denmark, Mexico, Spain and the USA.

Specifications

Span: 43.41m (142ft 5in)
Length: 45.87m (150ft 6in)
Engines: Series 10,20,30 -
    Four 55.3kN (12,500lb) to 77.8kN (17,500lb)
    Pratt & Whitney JT3C or JT4A turbojets
    Series 40 - Four 77.9kN (17,500lb)
    Rolls-Royce Conway R Co 12 turbojets
    Series 50 - Four 80.6kN (18,000lb)
    JT3D turbofans
Cruise speed: Series 10 900km/h (490kts),
    Series 50 933km/h (504kts)
Accommodation: Series 10,20,30,40 - 176 max
    Series 50 - 189 maximum

Originally delivered to Alitalia as a Series 43 in 1965, this DC-8 was converted to a Series 54(F) in 1978 and bought by AERAL. It was photographed at Milan Malpensa in June 1980. (Brooklands Museum Archives)

Seen at Miami International in October 1992 was this 1966-vintage DC-8-55F N807CK of Detroit-based Kalitta. The famous Kalitta family founded their freight airline in 1965 but currently trade as Kitty Hawk International. (Author)

This Fairchild-built F-27J was manufactured in 1965 for Allegheny Airlines. After three years service with Air South, N2706J went to Tahiti and later to France. (Bruce Drum)

FAIRCHILD F-27/FH-227

Fairchild Hiller Corporation
Germantown, Maryland
USA

In April 1956, an agreement was reached between Fokker in the Netherlands and the Fairchild Engine and Airplane Company at Hagerstown, Maryland that would allow the Fokker F.27 Friendship to be built and marketed in the USA under licence. The Americans realised that the modern short-range turboprop airliner was one that they could build and sell without all the expense of the initial design and test work. Fairchild's hopes that US domestic operators would place early orders was confirmed when sales were made to West Coast, Bonanza, Piedmont, and Northern Consolidated Airlines.

The first US-built Fairchild F-27 flew from Hagerstown in April 1958. The American FAA granted type approval in July 1958 and strangely it was a West Coast Airlines Fairchild F-27 which flew the world's first Friendship service, beating Aer Lingus's Fokker-built example by three months.

Although the Fairchild and Fokker-built aircraft were externally similar, there were actually many differences between the two. Indeed, they were so different that engineers needed separate manuals and a completely different stock of spare parts in order to maintain them. The Fairchild had different wheels and brakes, different air conditioning, more fuel capacity, American-built instruments, standard seating for 40 passengers and a longer nose to house a weather radar. This last device was later

adopted by Fokker, thereby removing the most obvious difference between the two types! More hard to spot external differences include the positioning of the pitot tubes. These were on the wingtips of the Fokker and on the nose of the Fairchild. One easy way to tell the two apart is to wait until the door opens; unlike the Fokker version, many Fairchild-built Friendships had a pneumatically operated integral airstair with the steps built into the back of the rear passenger door.

Fairchild versions include the F-27A and F-27J with uprated engines, the F-27B with a large forward cargo door (same as in the Fokker F.27 Mk.300 Combiplane), the F-27F corporate transport and the F-27M for hot-and-high operations.

Both companies worked on a stretched Friendship design in the mid-1960s. Fokker produced the F.27 Mk.500 with a 1.50m (4ft 11in) forward fuselage plug, while Fairchild, who in 1964 had merged with Hiller, independently produced the even longer Fairchild Hiller FH-227. This had a 1.83m (6ft 0in) fuselage extension plus various refinements incorporated especially for the US domestic market. The FH-227 first flew in January 1966, nearly two years before the F.27 Mk.500, and initial deliveries were to Mohawk Airlines.

Further versions of the FH-227 were built including the 56-seater FH-227B which was

certificated in June 1967, and the FH-227C, D and E with differing weights, propellers and engines. Altogether 128 Fairchild F-27s and 79 FH-227s had been completed when production ended in July 1973.

Currently, more than 20 airworthy Fairchild F-27s can be found in Central and South America with operators such as Aerocaribe, Aerogal and CATA. Likewise, a similar number of airworthy FH-227s can be found in the same areas with only a few others operating elsewhere. Due to the availability of Fokker products in Europe, very few Fairchild-built Friendships were used on the eastern side of the Atlantic. Currently, Marseilles-based Air Provence International operates two FH-227Bs as 48-seat airliners. No Fairchild-built Friendships appear to have been preserved.

Specifications

Span: 29.00m (95ft 2in)
Length: F-27 23.50m (77ft 2in) FH-227 25.50m (83ft 8in)
Engines: Two Rolls-Royce Dart turboprops, typically 1,282kW (1,720shp) RDa.6 Mk.511 in the F-27 and 1,700kW (2,250shp) RDa.7 Mk.532-7 in the FH-227
Cruise speed: F-27 439km/h (237kts) maximum FH-227 473km/h (255kts) maximum
Accommodation: F-27 44 max, FH-227 52 max

Compare the fuselage length of this Fairchild Hiller FH-227 to that of the Air South F-27J on the opposite page. Seen here at Jersey in August 1986, OO-DTE was operated by Belgian airline Delta Air Transport for nine years. (Author)

Very few FH-227s still operate in Europe. This 1967 model FH-227B F-GCLM was originally delivered to Ozark Airlines and is now flown by Marseilles-based Air Provence International alongside six Grumman Gulfstream 1s and a couple of HS748s. (Author's collection)

First airline to operate a Fokker-built Friendship on commercial services was Aer Lingus. This magnificent shot of EI-AKD was taken in March 1965 and shows the second colour scheme carried by their fleet. (Graham Simons collection)

FOKKER F.27 FRIENDSHIP

Fokker
PO Box 12222, NL-1100 AE
Amsterdam-Zuidoost, Netherlands

Until the arrival of the Airbus A320 family (1,000th delivered in April 1999) the Friendship was the best selling airliner designed in Western Europe, with a total of 786 built by Fokker in Amsterdam and Fairchild in the USA.

Around 1950, Fokker proposed their 32-seat Project 'P.275' as a DC-3 replacement. Unlike most of the designs which were planned to replace the trusty Dakota, Fokker's aircraft became a huge success; one reason for this was that it was designed around the best engine available at the time, the remarkable Rolls-Royce Dart turboprop. In 1952, Fokker completed their design and changed its designation to the F.27. With a capacity for up to 40 passengers and a 483km (300nm) range, Fokker hoped that it would prove strong competition to the American designs and hopefully win back the status that they had held between the two world wars with their successful series of civil airliners.

The prototype F.27 first flew in November 1955, and by the time the first production model, now christened 'Friendship', flew in March 1958, a boost for American sales had come from the Fairchild Company, who had commenced building the F.27 under licence at Hagerstown, Maryland. (See Fairchild F-27 on page 90). Note that the Fokker aircraft used a dot between the 'F' and the '27' and Fairchild used a dash! Early deliveries from the Fokker factory at Schiphol were to Aer Lingus,

Braathens SAFE and Trans Australia Airlines.

Initially the Fokker Friendship variants included the Mk.100 with Dart 514s and the Mk.200 with the more powerful Dart 532s. The Mk.200 first flew in September 1962. The Mk.300 'Combiplane' was similar to a 100 but had a large forward cargo door and strengthened floor for use in mixed freight/passenger mode. The Mk.400, also with the 532 engines, was designed primarily for military use. Fokker thought about a stretched Friendship for some time before they decided on a 1.5m (4ft 11in) stretch which created the 52/60-seater Mk.500. This first flew in November 1967 and remained in production until 1986. The quick-change Mk.600 which first flew in November 1968 had the 200 fuselage, the cargo door, and the stronger floor of the 300/400.

In the 1970s, Fokker began to promote their F.28 Fellowship in the USA. As the Fairchild 27/227 had ceased production, customers were also interested in acquiring new F.27s from Fokker. They sold several Friendships to corporate users in the USA, but the first for airline use were sold to Swift Aire in California and the last flown to the USA were actually the final Friendships built. In 1986 a batch of F.27 Mk.500s were delivered to Air Wisconsin, a remarkable 31 years after the F.27 first flew. In November 1983, Fokker launched their new Friendship replacement, the larger and more efficient Fokker 50.

Thanks in every way to the remarkable RR Dart turboprop, the Friendship can still be found in service all over the world. However, the advent of the new generation turboprops, such as the ATR42/72, ATP, Fokker 50 and Dash 8, will ensure that surviving Friendships will be further relegated to less glamorous aeronautical duties. Current passenger airline use in the west's major fleets is now low, but the following countries are still believed to fly passenger Friendships; Algeria, Angola, Australia, Bolivia, Brazil, Burundi, Cuba, Guinée-Bissau, Indonesia, India, Libya, Mexico, Myanmar, Pakistan, Peru, Philippines, Tanzania, Tchad and Uganda.

The second F.27 to be built was acquired for preservation by the F.27 Friendship Association in November 1995 and has been restored in Fokker's prototype colours. Many other early Friendships are still in service including the third one built. This aircraft is currently in Australia flying specialist tours, more than 40 years after it first flew.

Specificiations (for the Mark 500)

Span: 29.00m (95ft 2in)
Length: 25.06m (82ft 3in)
Engines: Two 1,279kw (1,715shp) to 1,730kW (2,320shp) Rolls-Royce Dart turboprops
Accommodation: 52 standard 60 maximum
Cruise speed: 474km/h (256kts)

Photographed at Hatfield six days after its first flight in 1970 is Fokker Friendship Series 600 PH-FPG. Later delivered to Royal Air Inter in Morocco, it is currently in service in Canada. (Author's collection)

Originally bought by East West Airlines of Australia in 1965, this F.27-100 arrived in Sweden via service in Norway. Gothenburg-based SWE Aviation Europe currently owns a fleet of five Friendships. (Author's collection)

Photographed by the late Peter Keating, Grumman SA-16 Albatross PK-OAH displays Airfast's lovely yellow colours at Seletar airport in August 1974. The company was founded in 1971 and still operates classic types such as the DC-3, HS748 and Turbo Mallard. (Peter Keating)

GRUMMAN G-64 & G-111 ALBATROSS

Grumman Aircraft Engineering Corp
Bethpage, Long Island, New York
USA

After the great success of their G-21 Goose, the Grumman Aircraft Engineering Corporation were encouraged by the US Navy to build a larger 'utility transport amphibian'. Design work commenced in 1944 incorporating many new refinements compared to the Goose. These included an all new low-drag fuselage, longer wingspan, a cantilevered tailplane and a fully retractable tricycle undercarriage. First flight of the XJR2F-1 'Albatross' was made on 24th October 1947. Initial use was purely military, with examples serving with the US Navy, Coastguard and Air Force. Most commonly known military designators were HU-16 and SA-16. The Grumman Albatross was given the company designator G-64 but despite their hopes for civilian sales, most operators found their G-21s to be more economical than the bigger and more fuel-thirsty Albatross. Between 1960 and 1968, Pan American operated two G-64s on behalf of the Trust Territory Air Services in Micronesia. These aircraft were given the nickname 'Clipper Ducks'.

Grumman built 464 Albatrosses and when the well maintained military examples became surplus to requirements in the late 1970s, several were offered to civilian operators as an upgrade to their trusty Geese (Gooses?). However, due to the high operating costs compared to the Goose, very few were purchased and Grumman were approached

by one company, Resorts International, with a plan to convert Albatrosses to commuter amphibians. Grumman purchased 57 ex military Albatrosses for conversion to civil G-111 configuration and the first one flew on 13th February 1979. However, despite the improved configuration and the airframe being 'zero-timed', the market for these aircraft did not appear and only 12 G-111s for Resorts International were completed. Main differences from the G-64 were the new passenger cabin with a galley, improved entry and escape doors and hatches, and an updated flight deck with the latest in solid state avionics.

By 1985, a subsidiary of Resorts International, Chalk's International, who advertised themselves as 'the World's oldest airline' were operating five G-111 Albatrosses from their Watson Island base in Miami. However, the type proved to be too big for their services and most of the G-111s were flown into storage leaving Chalk's to concentrate on their Turbo Mallards. One G-111 did survive with Chalk's until early 1996, when the airline changed its name to Pan Am Air Bridge.

A projected Albatross conversion with Garrett TPE-331 Turboprops and Dowty-Rotol four–bladed propellers was also researched by Grumman and Resorts International, but the aircraft was not built. In 1986 a further project was promoted by Frakes International.

Their proposal to update Albatrosses with either the PT6A or the PW120 turboprop also came to nothing.

Both the early G-64 Albatross and the upgraded G-111 version are now becoming hard to find. However, due to the Americans' love of 'warbirds', a few surviving Albatrosses are now appearing at airshows in full military colours while many more are preserved in genuine air force colours at museums around the world. One current commercial operator is Mirabella Yachts Inc from Fort Lauderdale in Florida. Their 19-passenger G-111 is available for charters.

Specifications (for the G-111)

Span: 29.46m (96ft 8in)
Length: 18.67m (61ft 3in)
Engines: Two 1,100kw (1,475hp) Wright R-1820-982C9HE3 Radial piston engines
Cruise speed: 382 km/h (206 kts)
Accommodation: 28

Founded in 1919, Chalk's proudly claimed that they were the World's oldest airline. In the 1980s they flew a large fleet of Grumman amphibians including this G-111 Albatross N115FB seen here at Fort Lauderdale in 1984. (EMCS)

Most of the surviving airworthy Albatrosses are now flown as warbirds. N97HU, seen here at Boundary Bay near Vancouver in February 1999, has been painted by its owner Jerry Janes in a smart RCAF colour scheme. It is the oldest Albatross flying. (Chris Mak)

Seen here retaining its old Ford Motor Company colours of orange and blue, Coleman Air Transport's 1967 Gulfstream 1 later served in the UK with Brown Air, Capital Airlines, Peregrine Air Services and Aberdeen Airways. (Author's collection)

GRUMMAN G-159 GULFSTREAM 1 & G.1C

Grumman Aircraft Engineering Corp
Bethpage, Long Island, New York
USA

In the mid 1950s, Leroy Grumman saw the need for a purpose built executive transport to replace the many Second World War military types which had been converted for business use. These noisy and hard-to-maintain types included conversions of the Lockheed Lodestar, B-25 Mitchell and Douglas DC-3/ C-47 Skytrain/Dakota. The resulting G-159 design, although built for executive use, did later operate for various airlines.

Starting in 1956, the initial design work was based on Grumman's piston-powered S-2F Tracker and TF-1 Trader naval aircraft. However, the availability of the Rolls-Royce Dart turboprop allowed Grumman to build a totally new design that was elegant, spacious, practical and far superior to any of the previous offerings. Advanced features included an APU for air-conditioning and start-up, and a forward airstair, the combination of the two allowing totally independent operations from remote sites. Standard layout was for a crew of two and up to 14 passengers seated in individual seats on either side of a central isle. The first flight in August 1958 was soon followed by deliveries to an incredible number of highly prestigious companies including Conoco, Dow Chemical, Ford Motors, General Electric, General Foods, Kodak, National Distillers, Texaco, Upjohn and US Steel.

Although nearly all Gulfstreams were built as executive transports, the FAA did certify

the type and a few were completed as 19/24-seater commuter airliners for Associated Airlines (Australia). Later in their careers, up to 30 G-159s were converted from business use to airline configuration.

Military examples included nine Gulfstream 1s supplied to the US Navy as the TC-4C Academe navigation trainer in 1966/67 and a VC-4A transport for the US Coast Guard in 1963. Production ended in 1969 after 200 G-159s had been built.

The basic fuselage cross section and window design of the G-159 was later incorporated into the highly successful G-1159 Gulfstream II executive jet. Remarkably, this shape has continued through the Grumman biz-jet series right up to the current Gulfstream V.

Ten years after production finished, the then owner of the design, Gulfstream American Corp offered a 3.25m (10ft 8in) stretched conversion for use by commuter airlines. Fitted with a lavatory and baggage compartments, the 38-seater Gulfstream 1C first flew in October 1979 but failed to gain significant orders, and only five were built. First delivery was to Burlington, Vermont-based Air North, whose inaugural G-1C service was on December 1st 1980 between Rochester NY and Washington DC. Other early G-1C operators were Air US of Denver, Colorado, Chaparral Airlines and Metro Airlines.

Several Gulfstream 1 survivors still give excellent service as business transports, particularly in the USA, and commercial operations continue in Canada, Colombia, the Dominican Republic, France, Hungary, Indonesia, Israel, Mexico, South Africa, Venezuela, the USA and the Democratic Republic of Congo. Some of these are in convertible passenger/freight configuration.

Specifications (for the G-159 Gulfstream 1)

Span: 23.92m (78ft 6in)
Length: 19.43m (63ft 9in)
Engines: Two 1,485kW (1,990hp) Rolls-Royce Dart Mk.529-8X or 8E turboprops
Cruise speed: 560km/h (302kts) maximum
Accommodation: 24 maximum

Originally operated in the USA as a VIP transport, this Gulfstream was later flown in the UK. I photographed G-BMSR at Teesside in August 1991 having had a very pleasant one-hour flight in it from Gatwick as Aberdeen Airways flight SM602. (Author)

In March 1999, two Gulfstream 1s, including this example, YV-989C, were awaiting delivery to new Venezuelan airline AeroPar at Opa Locka in Florida. The sale obviously fell through because they were still there in January 2000. (Avimage)

BOAC's Hermes 4 G-ALDU 'Halcyone' was converted to a Series IVA and bought by Blackbushe-based Britavia in 1954. Photographed at New York Idlewild in September 1959, this aircraft was scrapped at Stansted Airport in Essex in 1962. (Tony Eastwood Collection)

HANDLEY PAGE HERMES

Handley Page Ltd, Cricklewood, London, NW2 and Radlett Aerodrome, Hertfordshire England

Designed during the Second World War, the four-engined HP.68 Hermes 1 was a pressurised airliner of conventional design able to seat 50 passengers in tourist configuration. The tailwheel-equipped prototype was built at Cricklewood and transferred by road to Radlett for final assembly and test flying. Sadly, on December 3rd 1945, this aircraft crashed on its maiden flight killing two of the crew.

Despite the setback, work continued on the urgently needed military version of the tailwheel Hermes, the HP.67 Hastings, and this first flew without problems in May 1946. 147 Hastings of various marks were built for the Royal Air Force in addition to four Hastings C.3s for the Royal New Zealand Air Force. Examples of this long-serving transport can be found preserved in the UK at Cosford, Newark and Duxford.

In April 1947, BOAC ordered 25 HP.81 Hermes 4. These 63-seater airliners were to be powered by the Bristol Hercules 763 engine and have a twin-wheeled tricycle undercarriage. A second tailwheel Hermes with a 3.96m (13ft 0in) fuselage stretch (the same as the Hermes 4) was built for development flying and this was demonstrated successfully at the SBAC show at Radlett in September 1947.

In 1949, Handley Page built two examples of the turboprop-powered HP.82 Hermes 5 to an order from the Ministry of Supply. These

aircraft were flown extensively to test the feasibility of turbine power, but despite their excellent performance (cruise speed 560km/h [343mph]), the production version of the Hermes continued to be built with piston engines.

The first commercial service by a BOAC Hermes was from London to Accra on 6th August 1950, but the type only lasted in front line service for a couple of years before they were replaced by Canadair Argonauts. However, in 1954 BOAC's Hermes did manage a short re-appearance in scheduled service as a result of the grounding of the de Havilland Comets. After this, the Hermes fleet was sold and many of them flew trooping flights with operators including Airwork, Britavia and Skyways. A few non-British airline operators also flew Hermes aircraft for a short time. Kuwait Airways, Middle East Airlines and Bahamas Airways all leased examples from British owners in the late 1950s.

Further use in the UK was with Silver City Airways, Britavia, Air Safaris and Falcon Airways, but by 1962 most Hermes had been scrapped. The last operator of the type was Gatwick-based Air Links who bought three Hermes from Air Safaris in 1962, cannibalised two of them and flew the survivor, G-ALDA, for a couple of years. The world's last passenger Hermes flight was on 13th December 1964.

The sole surviving Hermes memento is the preserved fuselage of G-ALDG at Duxford. This wingless wonder served as a cabin trainer at Gatwick for British United and British Caledonian before it was given to the airport fire service for an even more worthwhile use. Thankfully they didn't burn this unique edifice, but merely filled it with smoke allowing them to practice the evacuation of injured passengers from a 'burning' aircraft. In January 1981 I witnessed the departure of the fuselage on an articulated lorry to a safe home with the Duxford Aviation Society.

Specifications (for the Hermes 4)

Span: 34.44m (113ft 0in)
Length: 29.55m (96ft 10in)
Engines: Four 1,566kW (2,100hp) Bristol Hercules 763 piston radials
Cruise speed: 444km/h (276mph)
Accommodation: 63-82

The ramp at Singapore in 1958 was host to Hermes 4 G-ALDY. This aircraft was first delivered to BOAC in January 1951 and was bought by Skyways in 1955. It was leased to MEA for four months and later broken up at Stansted. (Scott Henderson collection)

Looking rather ungainly on its home made undercarriage and with no wings or tail, Duxford's preserved Hermes fuselage G-ALDG is the last remnant of Hermes left in the world. In the 1960s, this fuselage was used by British United, and later Caledonian, as a cabin trainer at Gatwick. (Author)

This Herald 204, originally delivered to BUA at Gatwick in 1962, was leased back from Air Manila International by Handley Page for five months in 1966. It is seen here in immaculate condition at the 1966 Farnborough Air Show. (Author's collection)

HANDLEY PAGE DART HERALD

Handley Page (Reading)
Radlett, Hertfordshire
England

In the early 1950s, design work commenced on yet another replacement for the venerable DC-3. The Handley Page (Reading) short-haul airliner was revealed around 1953 as an enlarged version of the HPR.1 Marathon with triple tail fins and four Alvis Leonides 'Major' piston radial engines. This choice of powerplant was encouraged by the manufacturer's extensive market research with potential customers who were reluctant to accept the new, more powerful, turbine engines because of the supposed difficulty in maintaining them 'up-country'.

The tail layout was changed to a single fin and the HPR.3 Herald was launched in 1954. Two prototype aircraft were constructed with the 650kW (870hp) Alvis Leonides 'Major' engines, the first one making its maiden flight at Radlett on 25th August 1955. Handley Page gambled that the Herald's ruggedness and its' simple and easy to maintain piston engines would be sought after by those airlines looking to replace their Dakotas. However, the market research was wrong, and with the Dart-powered Viscount and Friendship on the market, the orders for 29 aircraft from Colombia and Australia were cancelled.

It became obvious to Handley Page that the Fokker Friendship (see page 92) with its similar layout and turbine engines, was going to be a very strong competitor for the piston-powered Herald. So, in June 1957, they

wisely withdrew the prototypes from trials and converted one of them to twin Dart power in less than a year. First flown in March 1958, the HPR.7 Dart Herald was bought by the UK domestic airlines, British European Airways, Jersey Airlines and British United Airways. Early foreign operators included Arkia, Bavaria, Eastern Provincial Airways, Globe Air, Itavia, Maritime Central Airways and Sadia.

Four Series 101 Dart Heralds were completed, followed by 36 Series 200s with a 1.09m (3ft 7in) fuselage stretch. A Series 300 was designed for the American domestic market, but like the proposed Series 500,600,700 and 800, none were built. However, eight Series 400s, designed for military use, were built for the Royal Malaysian Air Force in 1963/4. Most of these returned to the civilian market after retirement from the RMAF.

The production line was transferred from Woodley to Radlett in 1966, but all manufacturing ceased in 1968 after only 50 Heralds had been built. The Handley Page company collapsed in August 1969. By the late 1980s, only a handful of Dart Heralds were still in operation. The largest fleet, some of which had been converted to 'Super' Herald configuration with strengthened floors and an upgraded flightdeck, was based in Bournemouth for freight services with Channel Express, and it was this airline that

flew the very last Herald service.

Six examples of the Dart Herald are preserved in the UK at Bournemouth, Woodley, Duxford, Norwich, Elvington and Gatwick. Taiwan may still have an engineless Far East Air Transport Herald stored in Huilien County and in South America, the airline 'Aerovias' in Guatemala City has three Dart Heralds. Two are for spares and one is reportedly being restored to airworthiness. Unless the Guatemalans can get theirs airworthy, then the last Herald to fly was on 9th April 1999 when Channel Express finally closed the book on their long association with the Herald and flew G-BEYF to Bournemouth-Hurn Airport for preservation.

Specifications (for the Series 200)

Span: 28.88m (94ft 4in)
Length: 23.01m (75ft 6in)
Engines: Two 1,605kW (2,105shp)
  Rolls-Royce Dart 527 turboprops
Cruise speed: 440km/h (238kts) maximum
Accommodation: 56 maximum

Photographed at Southend in 1983 was Trans Azur Aviation's sole Herald Series 214 F-BVFP. Originally delivered to SADIA Brazil in 1966, this aircraft is currently in storage in Guatemala. (Author)

During its retirement ceremony, the world's last airworthy Dart Herald G-BEYF was photographed performing a spirited farewell flypast at its Bournemouth Hurn airport base on 31st March 1999. (Richard Hunt)

The very first Trident was Series 1C G-ARPA. Seen here at Heathrow in 1969, it first flew in 1962 but was not delivered to BEA until 1965. It was scrapped at Prestwick in 1976. (Author's collection)

HAWKER SIDDELEY HS.121 TRIDENT

Hawker Siddeley Aviation Ltd
Hatfield Aerodrome
Hertfordshire, England

The family of short-to-medium range Trident jetliners owes its birth to a 1956 British European Airways requirement for a 100-passenger airliner capable of 600mph over a stage length of 1000 miles. The de Havilland Company offered BEA their 111-seater DH.121 design powered by three 12,000lb Rolls-Royce RB.141 Medway turbojets. Innovative features included an 'all-flying' tailplane, a built-in APU and a nose undercarriage leg that was offset by 24 inches allowing sideways retraction. Although the airline was pleased with the layout, they considered it was too big for their purposes and in 1958 they requested a scaled-down version. This request, probably the most significant of many by BEA, forced de Havilland to re-design the DH.121 into a 101-seater with lower-powered Rolls-Royce Spey engines and a reduced range. This reduction in size suited BEA but it proved to be the sales downfall of the type in that it made it very difficult to sell to other airlines.

In February 1958, the DH.121 Trident project was officially launched when BEA signed a letter of intent to purchase 24 aircraft with an additional 12 on option. The first production HS.121 Trident 1C (the Hawker Siddeley Group took over de Havilland in 1960) made its maiden flight from Hatfield on 9th January 1962 and the first commercial service was London to Copenhagen on 11th March 1964.

Later, various improvements to the basic 'BEA' design were offered. These included more powerful engines, improved wing leading edge devices and a wider wing span. The resulting 115-passenger Trident 1E first flew in November 1964 and orders were won from BKS Air Transport, Channel Airways, Iraqi Airways, Kuwait Airways, Pakistan International, Cyprus Airways and Air Ceylon.

BEA's Trident 1Cs proved to be such poor performers that their crews gave them the unfortunate nickname 'Ground Grippers'. In 1964, further improvements including greater fuel capacity and more powerful Spey 512/5W engines created the 'long-range' Series 2E. This was bought by BEA, Cyprus Airways and the Chinese airline CAAC. The Chinese insisted on a four-crew cockpit, rather than the normal three, allowing them to include a navigator.

In 1966, BEA announced that they now needed a bigger Trident! Once again Hawker Siddeley modified the design by stretching the fuselage by 5.00m (16ft 5in), reducing the fuel capacity and most significantly, by fitting a fourth 'booster' engine of 2,381kg (5,250 lb.) thrust in the base of the fin. The 179-seater Trident 3B became the last production variant and 26 were built for BEA. Thanks to their Smith's 'Autoland' equipment, BEA's (later British Airways) Tridents became world famous for their ability to land in poor visibility.

British Airways ceased Trident operations in December 1985 and by 1992 the only examples in service were with the Chinese Air Force/China United Airlines. About ten Chinese Tridents are believed to have remained in service until they were finally grounded in 1994/95. In the UK, several retired Tridents were flown from Heathrow to airports for use as fire/rescue trainers, push-back/towing trainers or to allow new drivers to practise manoeuvring their vehicles up to an aircraft. Airports which received Tridents included Gatwick, Birmingham, Belfast, Teesside, Manchester and Glasgow. Some of these have now been broken up but preserved Tridents exist at Duxford, Cosford, Heathrow and Wroughton. China has preserved at least four, whilst Sri Lanka and Cyprus are still believed to have Trident wrecks rotting away.

Specifications

Span: 1C - 27.41m (89ft 10in). 1E - 28.95m (95ft 0in). 2E/3B - 29.90m (98ft 0in)
Length: 1C, 1E and 2E - 34.98m (114ft 9in) 3B - 40.00m (131ft 2in)
Engines: 1C, 1E and 2, three 43.8kN (9,850lb) to 53.2kN (11,960lb) Rolls-Royce Spey RB.163 turbofans. 3B had additional single 2,381kg (5,250lb) RB.162 turbojet booster
Cruise speed: 2E – 974km/h (525kts)
Accommodation: (maximum) 1C – 103, 1E – 139, 3B – 170

CAAC's Trident 2E G-BABP is seen here at Hatfield on the day before its first flight on 2nd June 1974. Note that it carries two registrations, the British one for test flights and the Chinese serial number 252 . (Author's collection)

The only Trident 2 to receive this style of British Airways colours was G-AVFG. The aircraft was withdrawn from use in 1985 but remains with BA at Heathrow for use by ground engineers as a training airframe. (Author)

One of the four IL-12s bought by CAAC in 1952 was still in service at Xian in 1985. Although 505 was scrapped, its sister ship 503 still exists at the Aeronautical School at Tianjin. (Author's collection)

ILYUSHIN IL-12

Ilyushin OKB
45 Leningradsky Prospect, Moscow
Russia

Around 1943, the Soviet government requested indigenous aircraft manufacturers to design a passenger airliner to replace the hundreds of Douglas DC-3 and Lisunov Li-2 aircraft which were operated throughout the Soviet Union. The design proposed by Sergei Vladimirovich Ilyushin was his first attempt at a passenger airliner. It featured an unpressurised circular cross-section fuselage with seats for 32 passengers, a tricycle undercarriage and four Tumanskii M-88 piston radial engines.

In the event, the IL-12 first flew on 15th August 1945 with two Charomskii Ach-31 diesel engines, but these were not successful and the prototype was soon converted to use the new and subsequently very successful Shvetsov Ash-82 radial engines. These 14-cylinder piston engines were developed from the famous Pratt & Whitney Twin Wasp and were built in the USSR, East Germany and Czechoslovakia. With these engines, it flew for the first time on 9th January 1946 and was revealed to the public in August of that year.

Test flying revealed some problems with the directional stability, and the single engine performance and control was considered to be very poor. To rectify these faults, various modifications were applied which included the fitting of a small fillet forward of the fin. Further changes included a more efficient de-icing system and the provision of a tail stand to support the fuselage while loading.

(It obviously fell on its tail without it!). Thus modified, the type became the IL-12B.

Other versions produced were the all-freight IL-12T with a large port-side cargo door and the military assault transport IL-12D which could accommodate 37 troops on canvas seats.

The IL-12, given the NATO reporting name 'Coach', entered Aeroflot service in August 1947. Despite extensive use, its poor performance caused the airline to reduce the seating to a maximum of 18, and it became a financial burden. Having been designed for internal use, it was a surprise to see Aeroflot commence international IL-12 services in 1954. Paris and Stockholm were the first western cities to see the IL-12 followed by Vienna late in 1955. Other IL-12 destinations outside the USSR were Beijing (Peking) and Tirana in Albania.

With design work on the improved IL-14 (see page106) complete, production of the IL-12 stopped in 1949. The total production run of the IL-12 has always been open to speculation and the figures published by various authors have in the past quoted totals of 200, 663, 2000 plus, and in excess of 3000! However, in 1998, the head of the Ilyushin design bureau stated that the total number of IL-12s produced was 839.

Foreign buyers of the IL-12 included China (4 civil and in excess of 24 military), Czechoslovakia, Poland and Romania.

Remarkably, an airworthy CAAC (China) IL-12 was still in service at Xian as late as 1985, but not surprisingly, there are no IL-12s currently airworthy. Preserved examples can be found at the Monino Museum in Russia, the Datang Shan Aviation Museum, Changping, and at the CAAC Aeronautical School at Tianjin. In February 1999 a very rare ex-Aeroflot IL-12 was discovered in nice condition at the Slavyansk Aviation Technical College in the Ukraine.

Specifications

Span: 31.70m (104ft 0in)
Length: 21.31m (69ft 11in)
Engines: Two 1365kW (1830hp)
  Shvetsov Ash-82FN piston radials
Cruise speed: 350km/h (217mph)
Accommodation: 27-32

Compare the forward observation windows on this Chinese Air Force IL-12 to the CAAC example on the previous page. 35141 is preserved in this smart colour scheme at the Datang Shan Museum at Changpin. (Mike Green)

The largest operator of the Ilyushin IL-12 was of course Aeroflot. One of the handful of survivors from their fleet is kept at the Slavyansk Technical College in the Ukraine. Despite the tattered tail fabric, it is in reasonable condition. (Peter Bish)

The IL-14 was a very rare sight at Gatwick airport. This East German-built VEB-14P was delivered to Malev in 1958 and in 1966 it brought the Hungarian football team to England for the World Cup. (Dave Howell collection)

ILYUSHIN IL-14

Ilyushin OKB
45g Leningradsky Prospekt, 125190, Moscow
Russia

With the IL-12 proving to be a poor performer (see page 104), Ilyushin's endeavours to improve the design evolved into the IL-14. The various problems encountered with the IL-12 were addressed, particularly the poor single-engined performance, the cockpit instrumentation, de-icing and fire suppression. The whole airframe was given an aerodynamic clean up; however, the basic IL-12 fuselage was retained but with a completely new wing with a revised cross section and a tapered trailing edge. New, more powerful, Ash-82T engines were enclosed in more streamlined nacelles, and the exhaust outlets were ducted over the wing to ejector nozzles on the trailing edge, similar to the Convair 240 (see page 58) which had first flown in 1947. Apart from the revised nacelles, the most obvious external difference between the types was the larger square topped fin and rudder on the IL-14.

The IL-14 first flew on 15th July 1950 and large-scale production was commenced in Moscow around 1953. First produced were the IL-14 military transports for the Soviet Air Force alongside the 18-passenger IL-14P (Passazhirskii/passenger) for Aeroflot. Like the Antonov An-2 (see page 14), the IL-14 proved to be a very adaptable aircraft. A huge variety of sub-types were constructed including VIP transports, navigation trainers, photo surveyors, glider tugs, fishery patrol, iceberg patrol, freighter and ambulance. One

of the sub-types to survive in service the longest was the Polyarniy/Polar version operated by Aeroflot. These ski-equipped aerial workhorses were painted in a vivid red and white colour scheme and a few could still be found serving scientists and explorers at both poles during the 1980s.

In 1955 the design was strengthened and stretched by 1.00m (3ft 3in) allowing an extra cabin window and seating for a maximum of 36, creating the IL-14M (Modifikatsiya/ modification).

Despite its shortcomings, the type became a huge export success and examples were sold in 31 countries. Further success abroad was guaranteed by the licence production of the type by Avia in Czechoslovakia and VEB in East Germany. Between 1956 and 1960 Avia built 203 'Avia 14s' of various sub types including a few examples of the pressurised Avia 14 Super. More than 50 Avia 14s were sold to the Soviet Union in 1957/58 out of a total of 127 Avia 14s exported. The VEB (Volks Eigene Betriebe) factory at Dresden in what was then the German Democratic Republic built 80 VEB-14Ps between 1955 and 1958. The majority of these were sold abroad to countries including China, Hungary, Poland and Romania.

The last commercial operator in Europe was probably the East German Civil Aviation Department with their VEB built example used for navaid calibration flights until 1983. This

aircraft was later flown to its birthplace at Dresden and preserved with the registration carried by the first VEB 14, DM-ZZB. Further afield, China was still flying scheduled domestic CAAC IL-14 services in 1991. Currently, a single IL-14M flies irregular services in Cuba for Aerocaribbean in Havana.

Preserved examples include an airworthy example at Krasnodar used for joy rides while other, non-airworthy examples can be found in Afghanistan, Albania, Bulgaria, China, Czech Republic, FSU, Germany, Hungary, India, Mongolia, Poland, Romania, Slovakia and in the USA.

Specifications (for the IL-14M)

Span: 31.70m (104ft 0in)
Length: 22.31m (73ft 2in)
Engines: Two 1415kW (1900hp)
 Shvetsov Ash-82T piston radials
Cruise speed: 320km/h (173kts)
Accommodation: 24-36

China General Aviation's Avia 14F '623' has now been scrapped, but in 1991 it was the pride of the fleet and beautifully painted. Note the large observation window behind the cockpit and the obligatory Chinese bicycle under the wing! (Author's collection)

Most old airliners are only fit for recycling and scrap; however a few manage to survive in one piece like this old Czech Air Force Avia 14 '3153' in use as a restaurant at Lemesany in Slovakia. Note its proximity to the main E50 motorway. (Peter Bish)

What can one say about this photo of Aeroflot's brand new IL-18D CCCP-75404 other than magnificent! Photographed at Heathrow in September 1966, the fate of this particular aircraft is not known. (Paul Huxford)

ILYUSHIN IL-18

Ilyushin OKB
45g Leningradsky Prospekt, 125190, Moscow
Russia

The first aircraft to carry the IL-18 designation was a 60-seat, four-engined piston-powered airliner with a distinctive round nose similar to the Boeing Stratoliner. This relatively unknown Ilyushin airliner first flew in July 1947 and although it did not enter production, a few prototypes did fly services commencing in 1948.

By the mid-1950s, the USSR was in need of a new high-speed mass transportation airliner with medium range and able to carry 75-100 passengers and operate from unpaved runways. Designer A Shvetsov, under team leader Sergei Ilyushin, was assigned to develop a turboprop-powered airliner that would match the performance of the Vickers Viscount and the Lockheed L-188 Electra. His new design used the same wing area and fuselage diameter of the piston-powered IL-18, but the power would come from four powerful turboprop engines. The prototype and the early production aircraft had four 2,985kW (4,000shp) Kuznetsov NK-4 turboprops, while all IL-18s built after aircraft No.21 had the Ivchenko AI-20 engine.

First flown from the factory airfield at Frunze on 4th July 1957, Ilyushin's elegant and long-lived IL-18 was originally known as the 'Moskva' and first entered service in April 1959 on the Moscow to Adler route. In October 1959 Aeroflot's first international service by IL-18 was flown from Moscow to London Heathrow.

More than 560 IL-18s (NATO reporting name 'Coot') were built at GAZ No.30 at Khodinka, near Moscow.

As with most airliners, various upgrades and modifications created additional variants. The first series was improved when the IL-18B was revealed. This had an increased maximum take-off weight (MTOW) and a reconfigured cabin seating 84 passengers. In 1961, the 90/100-seater IL-18V first appeared and this version gradually became Aeroflot's standard model. The IL-18D, which for some reason was originally designated IL-18I, first flew in July 1964 and had more powerful AI-20M engines and a longer passenger cabin created by moving the rear pressure bulkhead. This could seat 122 passengers, but only in the summer months when Aeroflot removed the winter-coat wardrobes. The IL-18E was similar to the IL-18D variant but had the same fuel capacity as the IL-18V.

Like its piston-powered forerunner, the IL-14, many IL-18s were exported to communist countries or those which were politically friendly to the USSR. Between 1960 and 1969, more than 100 IL-18s were delivered to foreign operators including Malev, Interflug, Cubana, Ghana Airways, United Arab Airlines, Air Mali, Air Guinée, CSA, Balkan, CAAK, LOT and Tarom.

Although the civil IL-18 production line closed around 1970, various military versions

based on the IL-18 continued to be built until the mid-1970s. The IL-20 is an ELINT/Reconnaissance aircraft, the IL-22 is an airborne command post and the IL-38 (NATO Code name 'May') is used for maritime patrol. A civil version of the IL-20 is the IL-24N used for fishery patrols.

In 1999 there were reported to be nearly 50 IL-18s still in passenger and/or freight service. Most of these are in the FSU, but other countries with flying examples include Cuba, Bulgaria, North Korea, Romania and the UAE. Thankfully for airliner enthusiasts, many examples of this reliable propliner have been preserved for posterity. You can find IL-18s in the FSU, China, Germany, Hungary, Bulgaria, the Czech Republic and Poland. Not all of them are museum pieces; some of them are in use as restaurants, cafes and ground trainers.

Specifications

Span: 37.4m (122ft 9in)
Length: 35.9m (117ft 9in)
Engines: Four 3,170kW (4,250shp)
Ivchenko AI-20M turboprops
Cruise speed: 675km/h (365kts) maximum
Accommodation: 122 maximum

Working in Gatwick Airport's control tower for many years allowed me the opportunity to catch many classic airliners on film. This is 105-seater IL-18E SP-LSF taxying outbound on to taxiway 8 in June 1989. (Author)

Thankfully, airworthy IL-18s can still be found with about 50 in commercial service, mostly with operators in the FSU. Here is one of Ramair's six IL-18s captured on film at Sharjah in March 1998. (Author)

Displaying its very early Aeroflot colour scheme at Paris Le Bourget in August 1969 is IL-62 CCCP-86662. Note the early wingtip design on this 1965 Kazan-built example. (Colin Ballantine collection)

ILYUSHIN IL-62

Ilyushin OKB
45g Leningradsky Prospekt, 125190, Moscow
Russia

In the early 1960s and amid the usual great secrecy, Factory No.22 at Kazan built the prototype of a new long-range jet airliner which was designed to complement and partially replace the long-range Tupolev Tu-114 turboprop airliner. The unfinished aircraft, known as the Ilyushin IL-62, was viewed by a group of Soviet leaders including the then Premier Khrushchev on September 24th 1962. This prototype first flew in January 1963 powered by four Lyulka AL-7 turbojets instead of the planned NK8-4 turbofans because the Kuznetsov engines had not been developed enough for test flying.

The first sight of this type in the West was when a Kuznetsov-powered prototype Ilyushin IL-62 was displayed at the 1965 Paris Air Show. Looking remarkably like the Vickers VC-10, the IL-62 was advertised as able to fly non-stop from Moscow to New York. The IL-62 suffered several long delays in its testing due to problems with the engines and with its low-speed handling caused by the 'T' tail. The fitting of huge leading-edge extensions to the outer wings eventually solved the handling problems. The type's first proving flight was from Moscow to Khabarovsk in February 1966 followed a year later by a regular freight service on the same route. The first true passenger service was from Moscow to Khabarovsk and Moscow to Novosibirsk in March 1967 followed by its first Aeroflot international service from

Moscow to Montreal on September 15th.

About 95 of the standard IL-62 (NATO reporting name 'Classic', appropriate for this book!) were built before the availability of more efficient Soloviev engines allowed Ilyushin to re-engine the IL-62 and add various improvements. The new variant IL-62M first flew in 1971and was displayed at that year's Paris Air Salon. With a 12% improvement in specific fuel consumption and a 5000 litre (1,400 US Gal.) auxiliary fuel tank in the fin, the IL-62M was able to fly non-stop from Moscow to Washington, thereby cutting out the tech stop at Shannon or Gander. Other changes included improved clamshell thrust reversers, a revised cabin, new cockpit avionics and various modifications to the wings and baggage holds. First IL-62M service was in 1974.

Further modifications to the IL-62M saw the higher weight IL-62MK launched in 1978. This has a stronger wing structure designed to increase the fatigue life, a further revised cabin interior with a wider aisle and overhead lockers, and a new main undercarriage with wider bogeys.

Nearly 90 IL-62s were exported to countries such as Angola, China, Cuba, Czechoslovakia, East Germany, Egypt, North Korea, Poland and Romania. Airlines such as CSA and Tarom have now withdrawn all their IL-62s and replaced them with Western built types, but the IL-62 is still easy to find in the

FSU where more than 100 operate with the major airlines there including Aeroflot, Air Ukraine and Domodedovo Airlines. Non-FSU operators currently include Air Koryo, Cubana and TAAG Angola. Several IL-62s are used as VIP transports in the FSU. These can often be identified by their immaculate paintwork and the extended dorsal fin which contains additional communications equipment.

A few redundant IL-62s have managed to escape the scrap man and have been preserved. In the FSU, a 1967-built Aeroflot IL-62 is preserved at the Monino Museum and another is on display in Ulyanovsk. The Chinese have preserved one at Datang Shan and a couple of ex-Interflug aircraft are preserved at Erfurt and Leipzig in the former East Germany. Cubana reportedly have one on display in Havana and at least two ex-CSA IL-62s survive including one in use as a restaurant at Lipa and another in a scrapyard in North Carolina complete with 'Super VC-10' titles!

Specifications

Span: 43.20m (141ft 9in)
Length: 53.12m (174ft 4in)
Engines: IL-62 Four 103kN (23,150lb)
   Kuznetsov NK-8-4 turbofans
   IL-62M Four 107.9kN (24,250lb)
   Soloviev D-30KU turbofans
Cruise speed: 900km/h (485kts) maximum
Accommodation: IL-62 186, IL-62M 198,
   IL-62MK 195

The IL-62 was obviously destined to feature in this book because the type was given the NATO reporting name 'Classic'! Here is CSA's IL-62M OK-JBJ tucking up its gear after departure from Zurich in 1992. (Author)

Not to be confused with Ukraine International, Air Ukraine's large fleet of mostly propeller types is capped by six Ilyushin IL-62Ms. Originally with Aeroflot, UR-86135 was built in 1987 and is based at Kiev-Borispol.(Rolf Wallner)

CASA 352L D-CIAS is seen here preserved at Frankfurt in 1974. Originally operated by the Spanish Air Force in the late 1940s, this aircraft is currently preserved at the new Munich Airport. It is hoped to paint it in early SAS colours during 2000. (Author's collection)

JUNKERS Ju 52/3m, CASA C352L, AAC.1

Junkers Flugzeug und Motorenwerke AG, Dessau Germany. Construcciones Aeronauticas SA, Madrid Spain. Ateliers Aéroanutiques de Colombes, France

First flown in 1930, the prototype Ju 52 was a single-engined freighter powered by a Junkers L88 radial engine. Much like the later three-engined Ju 52/3m, the Ju 52s were powered by a variety of different engines. For example, the Canadian Airlines Ju 52 which operated from 1931 to 1942 around the Hudson Bay had a Rolls-Royce Buzzard motor.

Poor sales, and a lack of trust in single-engined airliners, encouraged Junkers to adapt the design to use three engines. The seventh Ju 52 on the production line was converted to '3m' (3-motor) configuration, with three 410kW (550hp) Pratt & Whitney 'Hornet' radial engines, licence-built by BMW. No more single-engined Ju 52s were completed.

The large number of variants of the 3m which were produced over the years were matched by the variety of engines used. Deliveries commenced in 1932 and by the end of 1935, nearly 100 were in airline use around the world, half of them in service with Deutsche Lufthansa.

The ability of the sturdy Ju 52/3m to operate on floats, skis or wheels ensured that its military applications would be considerable. The Luftwaffe employed the vast majority as troop transports, while some were converted to bombers and glider tugs.

After a wartime agreement was made between the Germans and the Vichy Government in France to build 2,000 German

aircraft in occupied France; a production line for Ju 52/3mg10es was started at the former Amiot works at Colombes, northwest of Paris. There, they produced 415 aircraft which were later given the designation AAC.1 and the name 'Toucan'. Production continued after the liberation with the last one being delivered to the Armée de l'Air in 1948.

Under licence from Junkers, the Spanish company CASA built 170 after the war. Most of the CASA C352s were fitted with BMW engines, but 64 had more powerful ENMSA B3 engines built in Barcelona. The CASA 352 provided a long and reliable service to the Spanish Air Force and the last one was only retired in 1973. Post war, many major civil airlines operated the Junkers Ju 52/3m or licence-built examples. These included Aeroposta Argentina, Sabena, Lloyd Aereo Boliviano, Syndicato Condor (Brasil), CSA Czechoslovakia, DDL Denmark, Aero O/Y Finland, Air France, Iberia and AB Aerotransport Sweden.

Well over 40 examples of this long-lived workhorse are believed to exist. Of the airworthy examples mention must be made of the CASA 352 kept in airworthy condition by the South African Airways Historical Flight and the Ju 52/3mG.e which is flown by Lufthansa Traditionsflug in Hamburg. In addition to these, readers wishing to discover the pleasures of flying in a 'Tante Ju' are recommended to visit Dubendorf military

airfield in Switzerland. From there, the 'Ju-Air' company operates three original Junkers-built and one CASA-built aircraft on pleasure flights. In January 2000, Ju-Air's Junkers HB-HOS commenced a 40,000km round-the-world flight sponsored by the International Watch Company of Schaffhausen in Switzerland. By March it had reached Taipei and it was due back at Dubendorf at the end of May.

Other statically preserved examples and flyers can be found in Argentina, Belgium, Colombia, France, Germany, Portugal, Serbia, Spain, Sweden and the USA. In the UK there is an AAC.1 at Duxford and at Cosford a CASA 352L has been painted to represent a British Airways aircraft. Several ex-Luftwaffe aircraft have been discovered in Norway including some rescued from the bottom of a lake, but the best there is a float-equipped Ju 52/3M displayed at the Norsk Luftfartssenter at Bodo. The most remarkable 'Ju 52' preservation is in Winnipeg, where the Western Canada Aviation Museum has converted and restored a CASA C352L to single engine configuration to represent the Ju 52 of Canadian Airways.

Specifications

Span: 29.25m (95ft 11¼in)
Length: 18.90m (62ft 0in)
Engines: Three 541kW(725hp)
   BMW 132A-3 piston radials
Cruise speed: 240km/h (149mph)
Accommodation: 17

Commercially operated joy rides are available in four immaculately presented Junkers from Dubendorf airfield in Switzerland. JU-AIR has retained the former Swiss Air Force colours on this aircraft HB-HOT/A-702). (Hans Oehninger)

One of JU-AIR's Junkers (HB-HOS) is painted to advertise a well-known Swiss brand of chocolate. This machine would have looked wonderful parked next to the Pepsi Concorde! (Hans Oehninger)

After service with Kansas City-based Mid-Continent Airlines (later absorbed into Braniff Airlines) this Lodestar, NC25602, was operated by several private owners in the USA and one in Cuba. The aircraft survived in America until 1971. (Lockheed Martin)

LOCKHEED MODEL 18 LODESTAR

Lockheed Aircraft Corp
Burbank, California
USA

In its day, the Lockheed Lodestar was the fastest airliner in service around the world. Created by re-engineering and stretching (1.68m/5ft 6in) a 1937 Northwest Airlines Lockheed Model 14, the prototype Model 18 first flew on 21st September 1939 and had room for two extra passengers and a stewardess. Satisfied with their conversion, two more 14s were transformed into 18s before the first 'all new' 18 was completed and flown on 2nd February 1940.

Seven different models were offered, all with different engines, the most popular version being the Model 18-56 (C-60A) with 1,200hp Wright Cyclones. The first airline to buy them (at $85,000 each) and put them into service was Mid-Continent Airlines in March 1940. Despite the competition from Douglas's DC-3, many high profile sales were achieved to airlines such as BOAC, LAV, Canadian Pacific, Trans Canada, BWIA, TACA, Panair do Brasil, Pan American, Continental, National, East African Airways, Trans-Australia, New Zealand National, SABENA, and South African Airways. Some of these airlines flew Lodestar services both during and after the war.

Most examples flew in standard 14-passenger layout; however at least one was converted to carry 26 passengers on bench seats for operations in Puerto Rico. When production finally stopped in 1943, a total of 625 had been built, more than the combined total of all the Lockheed Model 10, 12 and 14s. More than two thirds of Lodestar production went to the US military forces with the most common variant being the USAAF C-60A 18-seat paratroop transport. Other designations include the R5O for the US Navy and Marines and the C-56, C-57 and C-59. Military Lodestar stocks were supplemented during the war with 100 civil Model 18s impressed into American and British service.

The final variant developed from the twin-finned 10,12,14,18 lineage was the slightly longer Lockheed 37 Vega/Ventura and Harpoon. Post-war, the Lodestar proved very popular as an executive transport and many were converted with uprated engines, retractable tailwheels, improved aerodynamics and plush new interiors. One company even converted them to a tricycle undercarriage. These conversions included the Minnesota Airmotive 'Super Lodestar', Bill Lear's Learcraft Conversions 'Learstar', the Dee Howard 'Howard 250', the Executive Aircraft Services 'Gulfstar' and the Dallaero Lodestar. In the USA, a few of these exotic machines still survive with proud owners who obviously prefer to arrive in style!

The world's last commercial operator of the Lodestar (PV-2) was Hirth Air Tankers in Buffalo, Wyoming. In 1997 they still had seven in use. Another late operator was the Finnish company Sir-Air. Their model 18-56 was equipped for aerial surveys and was appropriately registered OH-MAP. This aircraft still exists in a Finnish museum where it is currently being restored in wartime BOAC colours to represent an aircraft flown on clandestine operations from Scotland to Norway.

At least nine Lodestars are preserved in the USA and five in Canada. Others preserved include a genuine ex-SAA Model 18-08 which was 'rediscovered' after use by several civilian operators and is now maintained in static condition in original SAA colours at the South African Airways Museum. In New Zealand one survived for 24 years as a gate guardian at Gisborne Airport having served as a crop sprayer.

Specifications

Span: 19.96m (65ft 6in)
Length: 15.18m (49ft 9½in)
Engines: Two 540kW(750hp) – 895kW(1200hp) P&W Hornet, P&W Twin Wasp or Wright Cyclone radials
Cruise speed: 400 km/h (250 mph)
Accommodation: 14

Alaska Star Airlines' Lodestar 'Starliner Anchorage' had a short life. Based at Seattle in Washington State, NC21707 was cancelled in the late 1940s. Alaska Star was formed in November 1943 and became Alaskan Airlines in 1944. (Lockheed Martin)

The preservation of classic airliner types is very strong in South Africa. In addition to preserved types such as the Douglas DC-3, DC-4, Ju 52, Starliner and Viking, this beautiful static exhibit Lodestar ZS-ASN represents those used by South African Airlines. (Andy Heape)

Check out the classic airliners in the background of this June 1962 Heathrow photograph! Skyways' L-749 Constellation G-ANUR is taxying on two engines across to the south-side parking ramp with its undercarriage control locks still in place. (Author's collection)

LOCKHEED CONSTELLATION

Lockheed Aircraft Corporation
Burbank, California
USA

About sixty years ago, Lockheed proposed a new, pressurised four-engined airliner for long range civil use. The elegant Constellation was ready to fly in January 1943, but with the Second World War raging, the USA was in need of long-range military transports and the first 'Connies' built were quickly impressed into service with the United States Army Air Force as the C-69.

Months of aerodynamic research, including more than 500 wind tunnel tests, created the Constellation's distinctive and graceful fuselage shape. Apart from its obvious elegance, this curved design actually helped to generate lift. The Constellation design utilised the best and most modern materials; however, the rudder, elevators and ailerons were all fabric covered as this was still considered to be the best material.

After VJ Day, only 15 C-69s (from an initial order for 180) had been delivered to the USAAF. With the major post-war airlines crying out for their chance to operate the Constellation, Lockheed developed a programme to convert the C-69s into L-049 airliners. Orders for new production L-049 aircraft were pouring in and the early recipients, including TWA and Pan American, broke many records for transatlantic and transcontinental flights. Over the next few years, the world's national airlines, including BOAC, KLM, South African Airways, Qantas, Air France and Air India made the Connie their

flagship allowing them to significantly improve their flight times and reliability.

In May 1947, Eastern Air Lines introduced the new L-649 version which had been specifically designed for their medium range services. Only 20 of this high density 81-seater were constructed. Also revealed in 1947 were the long-range L-749 model with increased wing tankage and the L-749A with a stronger undercarriage. The L-749/749A series became the most numerous example of the Constellation with 125 examples built. An L-749 was used by Pan American to inaugurate the first 'Round the World' service in June 1947 and one military example became famous as President Eisenhower's VIP transport, 'Columbine'.

With the appearance of the Comet, Boeing 707 and DC-8, the Constellation was soon relegated to less glamorous roles. However, several Connies managed to survive into the 1970s and '80s as freighters particularly in Central and South America. By the late 1980s, the last enclave of working Connies was to be found in Santo Domingo in the Dominican Republic. On this oil-soaked ramp, various models, including Super Constellations (see page 118) could still be found operating services around the Caribbean and up to Miami.

Nobody flies Constellations on commercial services any more but about 15 of the 049/649/749 breed remain in existence,

mostly in the USA. Individual examples can be found in Morocco, Chile, the UK, France, Bolivia and Paraguay. The only airworthy ordinary (as opposed to Super) Constellation is in the hands of the Constellation Group of Scottsdale, Arizona. Their magnificent C-121A /L-749 N494TW is flown at airshows in full MATS colours and completed a very successful European tour in 1998. In 1999, a die-cast model of this aircraft was produced by Corgi Classics in the UK

Specifications (for the L-749)

Span: 37.49m (123ft 0in)
Length: 29.00m (95ft 2in)
Engines: Four 1620kW (2,200hp) Wright Cyclone R-3350 radials
Cruise speed: 480km/h (298mph)
Accommodation: 43

The last country to operate a significant number of Constellations on commercial services was the Dominican Republic. Aero Chago's L-749A HI-422 is seen about to depart San Juan in Puerto Rico in 1987. This aircraft was severely damaged in 1988. (Author's collection)

Air France sold this L-749A to Royal Air Maroc in 1960. After retirement it was hidden away in a hangar at Casablanca and used by engineering apprentices before eventually reappearing outside in fine condition. (Jacques Guillem)

This magnificent L-1649A Starliner was originally delivered to TWA in 1957. Converted to freighter configuration in 1960, it was operated by Alaska Airlines from 1962 to 1968. (Author's collection)

LOCKHEED SUPER CONSTELLATION & STARLINER

Lockheed Aircraft Corp
Burbank, California
USA

As the demand for air travel grew steadily after the war, airlines were keen to equip with aircraft which could seat more passengers and reduce their seat-mile costs. At the time, Lockheed were marketing their long-range L-749 model; however, the demand for larger aircraft saw them propose a stretched Model L-949 in 1948. Despite this aircraft's potential, it was rejected in favour of an even longer model, the L-1049 Super Constellation.

Lockheed modified the Constellation prototype to Super Constellation configuration in two stages at Burbank during 1950/51. Initial work consisted of the insertion of two constant-diameter fuselage plugs either side of the wing, thereby increasing the length by 5.59m (18ft 4in). Later, the round cabin windows were replaced by rectangular items, the outer fins were enlarged, the cockpit roof was raised and, for the flying trials one engine was changed to the definitive Wright R-3350-956C18CA-1 Cyclone. First flight was on 4th April 1951 followed by the first all-new Super Constellation in July. With its new fuselage extensions and the kink above the cockpit, it was still an elegant machine, but sadly it had lost the beautifully smooth curved lines of the earlier models. With a 40% increase in payload allowing accommodation for up to 92 passengers, the Super Constellation was ordered by Eastern Air Lines and TWA in April 1950. The first service was from New York to Miami by Eastern in December 1951.

Because they were rather underpowered, only 24 of the first version were ordered before the arrival of the incredibly powerful Wright Turbo-Compound engine allowed Lockheed to build the L-1049B and C versions with a significant increase of MTOW. The 1049C, first flown in February 1953 and initially ordered by KLM and TWA, was designed for civil use and had the 2,424kW (3,250hp) DA-1 Turbo-Compound engines. Despite this engine's poor reputation for in-flight shutdowns, Lockheed continuously upgraded the Super Connie for commercial use and sold large numbers to the US military as C-121s, R7Vs and WV-2s. Civil variants included the 1049D freighter and the famous 1049G 'Super G' with wingtip fuel-tanks. The final version was the convertible passenger/cargo 1049H in 1956.

Often described as the ultimate piston-engined airliner, the L-1649A Starliner was developed to compete with the Douglas DC-7C. Lockheed matched a strengthened L-1049G fuselage to a massive all-new wing of thinner cross-section which spanned 45.72m (150ft) instead of the previous 34.62m (123ft 5in). Along with the increased fuel capacity of 36,368 litres (8,000 gal) this gave maximum range of 10,170km (6,320 miles). However, by the time the first TWA Starliner service was flown from New York to London and Paris in June 1957, Boeing and Douglas, had both flown jet airliners prompting the airlines to

switch allegiance, leaving Lockheed with orders for only 42 Starliners.

Because of their temperamental engines and the advent of the jet, the Super Connie and Starliner had only a few years in front line service. As the major operators quickly switched to jets the 'Supers' and 'Stars' were sold to minor airlines or used as freighters.

Four Starliners survive, one in Johannesburg with the SAA Museum and three (one at Sanford FL and two at Auburn-Lewiston in Maine) with a true Starliner enthusiast, Maurice Roundy. He is determined to get one or more of them flying and has offered them for sale. The Super Constellation is in much better shape with preserved and stored examples (some ex-military) in Hermeskeil, Helena MT, Manila, Munich, Nantes, Penndel PA, Plonais (France), Topeka KS, Toronto and Washington DC. Flyable Super Connies are two at Camarillo CA, the 'Save a Connie' L-1049H at Kansas City and the Australian HARS C-121C at Bankstown. About eleven military Super Connies are preserved in the USA plus a couple of Indian Air Force 'Super G's in Pune and Agra.

Specifications (for the Starliner)

Span: 45.72m (150ft)
Length: 35.41m (116ft 2in)
Engines: Four 2,535kW (3,400hp) Wright 988TC-
    18EA-2 Turbo-Compound radial piston
Cruise speed: 550km/h (297kts)
Accommodation: 106

Originally built for the USAF as a C-121C, this Super Constellation eventually found its way to Aerolineas Mundo SA (AMSA) in Santo Domingo. After two years of service it crashed into the sea off Puerto Rico in 1990. (EMCS)

Another USAF C-121C which found a new life after years of storage at the Davis Monthan AFB is this beautifully restored Super Connie which is based in Australia with the Historic Aircraft Restoration Society. (John Mounce)

VH-RMA was delivered to Ansett Airlines in February 1959. Later converted to freight configuration, it was one of several Electras operated in the UK by Air Bridge Carriers and Hunting Cargo. (Lockheed Martin)

LOCKHEED L-188 ELECTRA

Lockheed Aircraft Corporation
Burbank, California
USA

Initial design work on the L-188 commenced in 1954 after American Airlines had posted a requirement for a short to medium stage airliner for use on domestic schedules. Designs by various manufacturers were considered and rejected until American altered their requirements allowing Lockheed to capture the order.

In June 1955, Eastern Airlines and American Airlines ordered a total of 75 L-188A Electras and Lockheed began production at Burbank with hopes of further significant sales. Indeed, their sales prospects looked good because by the time that the first Electra flew in December 1957, 144 had been ordered, including 12 for KLM in Holland.

The L-188 Electra (named after the earlier Model 10 Electra) was designed as a 100-seater which would be able to match the performance of the smaller Viscount by using bigger engines and an advanced wing. It was of conventional layout with a relatively short wing and engines that had their reduction gearboxes mounted separately behind the propeller. The L-188 Electra became the first and only significant turboprop airliner to be designed and built in the USA.

After the Electra's first revenue service was flown by Eastern Airlines from New York to Miami in January 1959, it became obvious that the type was popular with passengers and orders continued to arrive. All was not well however and Lockheed 's ambitions for

the L-188 were soon dashed from two sides. Because of the stage lengths that the Electra flew, it was in direct competition with other turbojet types including the new Boeing 707 and DC-8, and initial operating experience showed that the turboprop was not competitive on such long routes. The other, more tragic episode was when American, Braniff and Northwest Orient Airlines all suffered major Electra crashes within 15 months of them entering service. The FAA allowed Electras to continue flying, but until the cause was found and a cure applied, their speeds were severely restricted. A detailed examination of each wreck found the cause to be a structural failure in the engine nacelles. Subsequent strengthening and modifications to the nacelles, wings and propellers cured the problems, but the orders dried up, leaving Lockheed to complete only 170 Electras. The last one on the line was delivered to Garuda Indonesia in January 1961. The hugely successful P-3 Orion is a long-range maritime patrol version of the Electra. Over 700 were built, including some assembled in Japan. Some early examples have found new jobs as water bombers in the USA.

The initial variant, the L-188A, was followed by 55 Electras built to L-188C standard for Northwest Orient Airlines and Western Airlines. These had extra fuel tanks, higher weights and a 750nm increase in range. In 1968 the Lockheed Aircraft Service

Co started converting 40 Electras into L-188AF and CF freighters. Fitted with a reinforced floor and a large forward cargo door, the first order was for six conversions for Northwest Orient. Later orders followed from Western Airlines, Overseas National and Universal.

By the mid 1970s, the Electra had disappeared from front line passenger service, but the type was proving itself as a reliable and effective freighter in places like Australia, Colombia, Ecuador and the USA. Apart from a single Reeve Aleutian Airways aircraft in Alaska, all surviving Electras are believed to be pure freighters. The largest fleets in Europe belong to UK-based Channel Express and Atlantic Airlines. In Canada, some Electras have been converted into fire bombers while in the USA the large fleet that was operated by Zantop is up for sale.

Only two Electras are believed to be preserved. An ex-VARIG L-188A is at Campo Dos Afonsos in Brazil, the other is at an air base in Argentina. Dozens more are 'stored', especially in the USA.

Specifications

Span: 30.18m (99ft 0in)
Length: 31.81m (104ft 6in)
Engines: Four 2,800kW (3,750shp)
  Allison 501D-13A Turboprops or
  3,022kW (4,050shp) 501D-15
Cruise speed: 602km/h (325kts)
Accommodation: 99
Payload: L-188C/F 15,331kg (33,800lb)

The Electras which operated the 'Ponte Aerea/Air Bridge' service between Rio and Sao Paulo were always immaculate. L-188A PP-VJW made a great picture for Henry Tenby in September 1988. (Henry Tenby)

As the piston-powered water bombers became more expensive to operate, types such as the Hercules, Orion and Electra were modified to take their place. Conair's Tanker 53, Electra C-FZCS was photographed at Victoria International BC in September 1998. (Avimage)

This South East Martin 202A was photographed in July 1972. Originally 'Skyliner Los Angeles' with TWA, it ended its days at La Paz in Bolivia. Note the integral rear passenger stairs. (Bruce Drum)

MARTIN 2-0-2 AND 4-0-4

Glenn L Martin Company
Baltimore, Maryland
USA

Famous for the huge numbers of military aircraft it had built prior to and during the Second World War, the Martin company changed their policy post war by investigating the emerging civilian airliner market, leading to a proposal for a DC-3 replacement.

By late 1944, Martin had completed initial designs for the 30-passenger model 2-0-2. When this finally appeared in 1946, it had grown to accommodate 40 passengers, and was equipped with many innovative ideas including a rear airstair, reversible propellers and underwing refuelling points. The 'Martinliner' became the first post-war airliner design to reach production.

The 2-0-2 was ordered in quantity by Eastern and by Pennsylvania Central Airlines. Eventually Martin had orders and promises for nearly 300 2-0-2s and 3-0-3s (a pressurised version). First deliveries began in September 1947, but within a year virtually all orders were cancelled after a fatal crash of a Northwest Airlines 2-0-2. Subsequent investigations revealed that the wing forgings that had retrospectively given the 2-0-2 a 10° wing dihedral had failed catastrophically. Martin were forced to rebuild and strengthen every 2-0-2 in service. Only 43 Martin 2-0-2s were built.

In 1950, still determined to enter the airliner market, Martin announced the model 4-0-4. This was a pressurised 40-seater, externally very similar to the 2-0-2, but with a 0.99m

(3ft 3in) fuselage stretch, and a stronger wing design which was actually stressed to accept turboprop engines. The 4-0-4 was virtually a new aircraft in comparison to the 2-0-2; only 20% of the parts used were compatible with the earlier model. 101 4-0-4s were delivered to TWA and Eastern Airlines, while the last two 4-0-4s built were sold to the US Coast Guard.

By the 1980s, most of the surviving examples of this sturdy airliner had disappeared. However, various small operators scattered through North and South America managed to find uses for their 'Martinliners'. As well as operating passenger services, they were employed hauling freight, spraying crops and occasionally smuggling drugs! Quite a few were converted with a VIP interior including the currently airworthy example operated by 'Airliners of America' in California. Legitimate US operators in the '80s included Aero Virgin Islands, Marco Islands Airways and Air Florida Commuter. A handful found their way to Bolivia and TASS Bolivia still operated a 4-0-4 in 1990.

The only current commercial 'Martinliner' operator is Rentavion, based in Venezuela. Their two 4-0-4s are employed mostly on tourist flights to places such as Canaima. Other airworthy examples now belong to a new breed of preservationists who are keen to preserve civil airline heritage. For too long, the only large aircraft preserved were military,

but thankfully for airliner enthusiasts, museums and collectors are realising that there is a great deal of interest in this field. Preserved, flyable Martinliners survive in Pennsylvania, Kansas, Tennessee and California, while up to 20 others are stored, dumped or preserved, mostly in the USA.

Specifications (for the 4-0-4)

Span: 28.44m (93ft 3.5in)
Length: 22.75m (74ft 7in)
Engines: Two 1,790kW (2,400hp) Pratt & Whitney R-2800 Double Wasp radial piston engines
Cruise speed: 444km/h (240kts)
Accommodation: 40 (maximum 52)

After ten years of service with Eastern Airlines, N147S was purchased by Southern Airways in 1962. Seen in 1978, she was later flown by a variety of operators including Florida Airlines, Ocean Airways and Southern International Airways. (Author's collection)

One of only three flyable Martinliners is Camarillo-based N636X. Jeff Whitesell and his team at Airliners of America have painted the aircraft in authentic 'Pacific Air Lines' colours for the US airshow circuit. (Author)

Photographed a few days after it was delivered to Brazil in March 1968, Cruzeiro's YS-11A-202 PP-CTE first flew in December 1967. It was returned to Japan where it was operated by TOA Domestic Airlines from 1979. (Author's collection)

NAMC YS-11

Nihon Aeroplane Manufacturing Co Ltd
Toranomon Building, No.1, Kotohira-cho
Shiba, Minato-ku, Tokyo, Japan

Around 1956, the Japanese Ministry of International Trade and Industry offered a government subsidy to six high-profile Japanese companies to encourage them to jointly prepare and evaluate a short/medium haul airliner design which could be produced indigenously. The Japanese manufacturers certainly had the skills and facilities to build such an aircraft and the domestic airlines were in need of new equipment to expand services and replace piston-powered types.

The companies, Mitsubishi Heavy Industries, Kawasaki Aircraft Co, Fuji Heavy Industries, Shin Meiwa, Nippi and Showa Aircraft formed the NAMC (Nihon Aircraft Manufacturing Company) in May 1957 specifically to build the new aircraft with each company taking responsibility for a specified part. The major production partners were to be Mitsubishi and Kawasaki. Mitsubishi were responsible for the forward fuselage and the final assembly, Kawasaki the wings and engine nacelles. Design work on the NAMC YS-11 began in 1959 and with no suitable Japanese engine, the group chose the most powerful Rolls-Royce Dart turboprop in preference to the Allison 501 or the Napier Eland.

Construction of two prototypes commenced in March 1961 followed by a successful first flight in August 1962. Like the smaller but similarly laid out HS748, the engines were mounted forward and above the wing in large nacelles which also housed

the main undercarriage legs. The circular cross-section fuselage was pressurised and front and rear airstairs were provided on the standard passenger version.

Initial deliveries to Japanese airline and military operators began in March 1965. TOA Airways (now Japan Air System) began regular YS-11 services in April 1965. By late 1966 NAMC had won some export orders and a small number were built and delivered to Hawaii and the Philippines. The YS-11 was never in high demand, but by the mid-1970s steady sales and further exports found the type in service on every continent except Australia. Operators at this time included Olympic Airways, Piedmont Airlines, Cruzeiro do Sul and Transgabon.

After 49 of the original YS-11s had been built, production switched to the higher weight YS-11A in 1967. The YS-11A was offered in three versions known as Series 200, 300 and 400, causing the original YS-11 to be retrospectively called the Series 100. First delivery from this series was a YS-11A-200 to Piedmont Airlines in June 1968. Further versions included the 'Combi' YS-11A-300 and the all-freight YS-11A-400, both with large cargo doors. The final series offered were the heavier YS-11A-500, 600 and the unbuilt 700.

The last YS-11A delivery was in February 1974 to the Japanese Self-Defence Force. They currently operate about 20 YS-11s for

a multitude of uses including VIP/ECM/calibrator/training/ASW training and tactical transport.

Although the type has proved to be reliable and safe, the YS-11 cannot be considered a financial success. Its production costs and disappointing sales caused NAMC to make a loss of $600 million. However, the YS-11 is still in operation 31 years after its first service. Scheduled passenger YS-11 services are still flown in Japan by Japan Air Commuter and Air Nippon, but they are now withdrawing examples of this long-lasting airliner in large numbers. In Trinidad and Tobago, Air Caribbean currently operate a small fleet of 60-seaters and despite the threat to replace them with Boeing 737s, they will continue in service in 2000. In the Philippines, three companies operate YS-11s on freight and passenger.

The handful of YS-11s that are preserved in Japan include the prototype which is on display at the Narita museum. Other civil examples are stored in the USA and Mexico.

Specifications

Span: 32.00m (105ft 0in)
Length: 26.30m (86ft 3in)
Engines: Two 2,280kW (3,060shp)
  Rolls-Royce Dart Mk.542-10K turboprops
Cruise speed: 478 km/h (253kts) maximum
Accommodation: 60
Maximum payload: 6,670kg (14,704lb)

Originally delivered to Piedmont Airlines in North Carolina in 1970 with the name 'Peachtree', YS-11A-205 N273P is seen here at Barnstaple Municipal Airport on Cape Cod in 1988 wearing Provincetown-Boston Airline colours. (Author)

In the mid-1980s, Hawaiian operator Mid Pacific Air had a large fleet of YS-11s. Several were used as freighters including this example which was sold and later seen with Global Aircargo titles at Sharjah in October 1998. (Author's collection)

Prototype Nord 262 F-WKVR wore temporary Lake Central colours in 1963. Originally built without the production standard dorsal fin, this aircraft was later operated by the French Air Force. Lake Central Airlines ordered eight Nord 262s with options on a further thirteen. (Graham Simons collection)

NORD 260, NORD 262 & MOHAWK 298

Aérospatiale, 37 Boulevard de Montmorency, F-75781 Paris Cedex 16, France

Like many airliners, this design evolved from an earlier version which was enlarged and updated with the latest engines. The unique 1957 Avions Max Holste MH.250 Super Broussard was a high-wing piston-powered feederliner with 22 seats and a neat tricycle undercarriage in which the main wheels retracted into fairings on the fuselage. This design was improved by stretching the square section fuselage by 1.39m (4ft 7in) and fitting Turboméca Bastan turboprop engines. The resulting MH.260, also called the Super Broussard, first flew in July 1960.

In November 1960, the production, sale and development of the MH.260 design was taken over by Nord-Aviation who built ten production aircraft as the Nord 260. These aircraft were leased to Wideroe Flyveselskap in Norway and Air Inter in France for commuter operations. However, their civilian use did not generate sales and the aircraft were transferred to military service. At least four Nord 260s survived until the mid-1990s in French military service and one MH.260 is currently preserved at Le Bourget whilst another was still flying as a 'hack' with the Turboméca Company in 1996.

Nord-Aviation continued with design changes and in 1962 they revealed the new Nord 262 commuter transport. This 29-seater had a much longer all-new pressurised circular cross-section fuselage with three-abreast seating and more powerful Bastan VI

engines. The prototype 262, which first flew on 24th December 1962, was followed by three pre-production aircraft built at Chatillon-sous-Bagneux and assembled and flown from the test site at Melun-Villaroche. Production versions of the 262, built at Bourges, were ordered by various airlines including Air Ceylon, Air Inter, Alisarda, Cimber Air, Lake Central Airlines, Japan Domestic Airways, Linjeflyg and Rousseau Aviation. The French Navy and Air Force also ordered the type for light transport, communications and as a multi-engine trainer.

On the 1st January 1970, the Nord-Aviation, Sud-Aviation and SEREB companies were merged by the French government to create Aérospatiale. They built the 262C Frégate version with extended wingtips, extended tailplanes and more powerful Bastan VII engines. The military version, the 262D Frégate, was designed for the French Air Force.

In 1974, the US commuter airline Allegheny ordered its subsidiary Mohawk Air Services to upgrade its fleet of nine Nord 262s. The modifications included replacing the Bastans with 880kW (1,180 shp) Pratt & Whitney PT6A-45 turboprops with five-blade propellers, a new APU, new wingtips and the latest cockpit avionics. The resulting Mohawk 298 was so named because of the American FAR Part 298 airworthiness regulations which applied to the aircraft. The first of the 'new' aircraft flew in January 1975.

At least 26 Frégates still operate with the Armée de l'Air in France, but civil operations have virtually stopped. No Mohawk 298s are currently flying and until recently, commercial services with the few remaining Nord 262s were confined to Colombia, Guatemala and the Democratic Republic of Congo. Stored and derelict examples exist in France, USA and Australia.

Specifications (for the Nord 262)

Span: 22.60m (74ft 2in)
Length: 19.28m (63ft 3in)
Engines: Two 843kW (1130shp)
Turbomeca Bastan VIIC turboprops
Cruise speed: 408km/h (220kts)
Accommodation: 26

Lake Central's second Nord 262 was sold to Air Algérie in 1970 and in 1981 it was sold with three other Algerian examples to Limoges-based Air Limousin. It was photographed at Gatwick in May 1982. (Author)

One of the last passenger Nord 262s in use was TG-ANP in Guatemala. Seen here in service at La Aurora airport with Aerovias in 1995, it was bought by a new Guatemalan airline RACSA in 1998. (Pierre-Alain Petit)

This Saab 90A-1 Scandia PP-SQZ was originally delivered to Scandinavian Airlines System in 1954. Bought by VASP in 1958, it was photographed at Congonhas in November 1960 where it was eventually broken up in 1965. (Peter Keating)

SAAB 90 SCANDIA

Svenska Aeroplan AB
Linkoping
Sweden

Designed in 1944 by a team led by Mr F Likmalm, the attractive Scandia airliner was originally known as 'Project CT'. The all-metal, unpressurised design was later designated SAAB 90 and the appropriate name was chosen by staff who had entered a 'name the plane' competition.

When completed in the autumn of 1946, the prototype Scandia revealed its remarkable similarity to the Soviet Ilyushin IL-12 which was also under development at the time. Fitted with old-fashioned oval shaped cowlings around the two 1081kW (1,450hp) Pratt & Whitney R-2000-2SDI3-G engines and three-bladed propellers, it first flew on 16th November 1946.

With so many inexpensive war-surplus Douglas C-47 Dakota/Skytrains available, the all-new Scandia found little interest with the airlines in Europe and at home. Despite a rigorous series of demonstration flights carrying representatives of many of the major European airlines in 1947 and early 1948, no airline orders materialised until seventeen months after the first flight. In April 1948, an order from AB Aerotransport (Swedish Air Lines) for ten Scandias allowed SAAB to lay out a production line for a short series of aircraft. A later order for Scandias from Brazil was deemed by SAAB to be more important than the Swedish one, and the early production aircraft, now with more powerful engines, four-bladed props and circular

cowls, were re-directed to Aerovias Brasil and VASP.

By 1952, Saab's order book was full of high priority J.29 jet fighters for the Swedish Air Force and Safir trainers. This caused them a problem because there was simply not enough room for the Scandia production line to continue at the Linkoping factory. When an order for four Scandias was received from VASP in June 1952, Saab struck a deal with the Dutch manufacturer Fokker to transfer the production line to Holland. Saab had built twelve Scandias at Linkoping, including the prototype, but the last six were completed in Holland. By the end of 1954, the Dutch production line was closed, and grateful for the experience gained, Fokker went on to design and built the world class F.27 Friendship. (See page 92). Despite the original Saab plans to market both pressurised (90B) and unpressurised (90A) versions, in the end only the 90A variant was built.

Scandinavian Airlines Systems operated their Scandias from 1950 until 1957 when their fleet was sold to VASP along with the refurbished prototype. This created an almost unique situation in airliner production where every one built was at some time operated by a single airline in one country, VASP in Brazil.

By 1964, only six Scandias were still in service, all of them with VASP. They were almost solely used on the famous 'air-bridge' service linking Rio de Janeiro and Sao Paulo.

The world's last airworthy Scandia landed at Sao Paulo in July 1969 after operating a pleasure flight over Londrina and Maringa.

The Scandia can stake its claim for entry in this book because a single example, the last to fly, still exists in Brasil. After retirement, PP-SQR was moved to the 'Museu de Armas e Veiculos' at Bebedouro, 360km (200 miles) northwest of Sao Paulo in Brazil. This remarkable museum was based around a private collection of 82 motor cars dating from 1904, but it also had locomotives and military equipment as well as the Scandia, a Viscount, Convair 240, Commando, DC-3, DC-6 and Lodestar. In 1999 it was announced that the collection would be moved to a new site at Americana on the outskirts of Rio.

Specifications

Span: 28.00m (91ft 10½in)
Length: 21.30m (69ft 10½in)
Engines: Two 1342kW (1,800hp)
　Pratt & Whitney R-2180-E1 Twin Wasp radials
Cruise speed: 391km/h (242mph) maximum
Accommodation: 24-32. Maximum 36

Illustrations of any Scandia, especially SAS aircraft, are very difficult to find in colour. This late 50s half-frame Agfacolor slide of VASP's PP-SQQ in an early colour scheme is very rare. (Tony Eastwood collection)

An announcement was made in August 1999 that the collection of classic airliners at Bebedouro (200 miles north-west of Sao Paulo) would be moved to a new site at Americana near Rio. This shot shows the cramped conditions at Bebedouro with Scandia PP-SQR in 1979. (Author's collection)

One of only four ST-27s to be operated outside Canada, HK-1286 was originally built as the prototype ST-27 and first flew in May 1969. Medellin-based Colombian third-level operator ACES began operations in February 1972 with an ST-27 and eventually operated three. (Author's collection)

SAUNDERS ST-27

Saunders Aircraft Corp Ltd
Gimli, Manitoba
Canada

Of the 148 de Havilland Herons built, (see page 72), more than 30 were successfully upgraded by companies who converted them to Lycoming or Continental power. Connellan Airlines in Australia and Executive Air Engineering at Coventry, UK both converted a small number of Herons, but the most famous conversions were completed by Florida-based Riley Aeronautics. Their four-engined Riley Herons with turbo-supercharged Lycomings were highly praised and many of them lasted for years in service with airlines such as Prinair in Puerto Rico. However, despite the valuable increase of performance and reliability that these conversions gave to the Heron, in 1968 a group of Canadians felt that further improvements could be gained by re-engining Herons with two turboprops. A new company, The Saunders Aircraft Corporation, was set up in Canada expressly to convert Herons to Pratt & Whitney turboprop power. The Saunders ST-27 became the ultimate Heron.

Saunders bought some Series 2 Herons and after they were dismantled and inspected, remanufactured them using two PT-6A turboprops instead of the four original Gipsy Queen piston engines. Modifications to the airframe involved the fitting of a stronger redesigned main spar and the lengthening of the fuselage by the insertion of newly built plugs. Because of the additional passenger seating, extra emergency exits and a starboard side passenger door were also provided. The extra side profile from the longer fuselage required the fitting of an enlarged rudder, while the tailplane and undercarriage remained standard Heron. The prototype ST-27 first flew on 28th May 1969.

A dozen conversions were completed and sold to airlines in Canada and Colombia. By the mid-1980s, the largest operator of the remaining examples was the Canadian airline, City Express, based at Toronto Island Airport, Ontario. This airline, previously known as Air Atonabee, purchased eleven of the available ST-27s in the late 1970s, including the three examples which had been sold to ACES Colombia.

Eventually, a shortage of suitable Herons led Saunders to make plans for a completely new aircraft based on the ST-27. One Heron, originally delivered to the South African Air Force, was used as the prototype for the ST-27A. This involved the replacement of the tail fin, a new interior, extra fuel tankage and uprated PT-6A engines. Providing sufficient orders could be obtained, Saunders planned to build the ST-27A using all-new materials. The ST-27A designation was later amended to ST-27B, but in February 1975 it was once again re-designated as the ST-28. In early 1976, company financial problems forced Saunders to stop all work on the 'all new' ST-28, even though they had secured airline orders for more than 30 aircraft.

The ST-27 is no longer in service; however a handful have survived including the unique ST-28 C-GYAP-X which first flew on 12th December 1975. This aircraft was grounded after the company's problems, having made its last flight on 28th April 1976. It is presently stored at Gimli Airport in Manitoba while a decision is made on its future by its owners, the Western Canada Aviation Museum.

Awaiting restoration and display at this impressive museum is the sixth ST-27 C-FLOL. This was one of three examples given to the Canadian Bushplane Heritage Centre at Sault Ste Marie, Ontario, by the former operator Voyageur Airways around 1990. The CBHC swapped C-FLOL with WCAM for a Fairchild Husky and gave another one to the local Sault College as an instructional airframe. They kept the third one, C-GCML, and moved it by road from Ontario to Sault in 1994 where it is now on display inside a hangar.

Specifications

Span: 21.79m (71ft 6in)
Length: 17.98m (59ft 0in)
Engines: Two 560kw (750shp) PWC PT-6A-34 turboprops
Cruise speed: 338km/h (182kts)
Accommodation: Maximum 24, normally 20

C-FCNX, the eighth ST-27 was used in Canada from 1975 until it was retired in 1988 at Toronto Island Airport. Ontario-based Voyageur Airways had three ST-27s in 1985 including this example which was originally built as a Heron for the Kuwait Air Force. (Pierre Langlois)

Until 1984, Toronto Island-based City Express were known as Air Atonabee. They operated a total of seven ST-27s between 1979 and 1988. C-FJFH was originally Heron G-AOGU with Cambrian Airways. (Author's collection)

Not many enthusiasts made the journey to Kathmandu in the 1960s. Fortunately for you readers, Harry Holmes passed through Nepal in October 1968 and shot this rare Nepalese Royal Flight Twin Pioneer undergoing maintenance. (Harry Holmes)

SCOTTISH AVIATION TWIN PIONEER

Scottish Aviation Ltd
Prestwick Airport, Ayrshire
Scotland

Despite the connotation implied in the name, the Twin Pioneer is not a two-engined version of a Pioneer. The original Prestwick Pioneer was a high-wing STOL five-seater powered by a single Alvis Leonides piston engine. The 'Twin Pin', as it is affectionately called, was a completely new design, though it did use the Pioneer's outer wing panels and the same basic Leonides engines.

Designed for both civil and military use, its huge triple tail fins, long-travel undercarriage and genuine STOL capability ensured that this remarkable little aircraft was easy to fly and was capable of landing in a very short distance. The prototype was constructed at the Prestwick factory and first flew on 25th June 1955. A successful series of flight trials culminated in a brilliant display at the 1955 Farnborough Air Show where the little polished-metal airliner in Scottish Aviation titles showed-off its impressive 130m (420ft) take-off roll. The initial interest from potential customers was very encouraging for Scottish Aviation, prompting them to estimate a production run of 200 aircraft. Two early examples were subsequently sent on extensive worldwide sales tours.

First flown in April 1956, the basic version available was the Series 1 with 418kW (560hp) Leonides engines. In 1958 the Series 2 was offered with Pratt & Whitney's famous 447kW (600hp) Twin Wasp radial engines, but only a few were built to an order from

Philippine Airlines. The Series 3, which first flew in 1959, had the most powerful engines which gave an increase in all-up weight thereby allowing the carriage of extra fuel or payload.

Despite the early promise, airline orders proved hard to come by. Borneo Airways, De Kroonduif (a KLM subsidiary in Dutch New Guinea) and Philippine Airlines did place orders but most sales came in ones and twos. The Royal Malaysian Air Force bought 14 but the Twin Pioneer's biggest customer was the Royal Air Force who ordered 32 Twin Pioneer CC.1s and 7 CC.2s for use in Aden and in the Far East. They used their Twin Pins to carry medical evacuees, 11 paratroopers, 13 fully armed soldiers or 1,519kg (3,350lb) of freight. They could also be employed as a light bomber carrying up to 907kg (2,000lb) of anti-personnel bombs mounted externally, but more often they dropped supplies rather than bombs. British military service commenced in 1958 and the type was finally withdrawn in 1968.

Because the Twin Pioneer was a stable platform and could operate from unprepared strips, the type was often used for aerial mapping and geophysical surveys. Both the Swiss and Austrian governments operated Twin Pins with camera hatches as surveyors, and the famous Rio Tinto company had a specially adapted Series 1 with large fibreglass wing tip pods housing transmitting

and receiving coils for an airborne magnetometer.

Commercial operations in the UK only commenced in 1971 when Portsmouth-based JF Airlines bought two ex-Borneo Airways aircraft for services to the Channel Islands. After a couple of years the Twin Pins were sold to Flight One at Staverton who eventually obtained a small fleet, mostly for Ordnance Survey work for the UK Government.

Surviving examples of this rugged STOL airliner are spread throughout the world. Four complete examples exist in the UK, Australia has three, Malaysia has two, and Switzerland and Canada have one each. The only current 'flyers' are in the UK and Australia. At Coventry in the UK, Atlantic Airlines keep an airworthy example for pleasure flights and at Coolangatta, Queensland, Australia, Sherwell Aviation keep two for charter work.

Specifications (for the Series 3)

Span: 23.33m (76ft 6in)
Length: 13.80m (45ft 3in)
Engines: Two 475kW (640hp)
 Alvis Leonides 531/8 piston radials
Cruise speed: 210km/h (114kts)
Accommodation: 16

I well remember my scheduled flight from JF Air's Portsmouth base to the Channel Islands in this Twin Pioneer in August 1971. Their two Twin Pins were later repainted , one red, one yellow, before they were both sold to Flight One in October 1972. (Paul Wakefield)

Sherwell Aviation at Coolangatta, Queensland, Australia maintain this immaculate Twin Pioneer Series 3 VH-AIS. With seats for 16 passengers, it is used for tourist charters and carries the inscription 'Fly Twin Pion Air' (Craig Justo, Aero Aspects)

Taken in October 1964, this shows Ansett Flying Boat Services' Short Sunderland 5 VH-BRF at the Rose Bay mooring near Sydney. Ansett converted this aircraft from a RNZAF Sunderland to Sandringham standard in 1963. (Author's collection)

SHORT SUNDERLAND/SANDRINGHAM/SOLENT

Short Bros (Rochester and Bedford) Ltd, Seaplane Works
Rochester, Kent and Windermere, Cumberland. Short Bros
and Harland Ltd, Queens Island, Belfast, Northern Ireland

Twenty-seven Bristol Pegasus-powered Sunderland 3s were civilianised for joint BOAC/ RAF Transport Command transport duties from 1943. Flown by BOAC crews, these camouflaged flying boats carried the famous 'Speedbird' emblem as well as huge civil registration letters underlined with red, white and blue stripes. First employed on the West Africa route, they carried mail and government-sponsored passengers in their sparsely equipped and noisy cabin on uncomfortable bench seats. All armament was removed, the tail gun position was completely faired over, and the retractable nose turret was replaced by a similar shaped fairing. After VE day these aircraft were given proper civilian colours and were gradually upgraded to carry 24 day/16 night passengers. Known to BOAC as the 'Hythe' Class, they had very meagre passenger facilities but they did re-open the old 'Empire' routes that were so famous pre war.

In 1945, one aircraft, 'Himalaya', was returned to Rochester and after extensive remodelling emerged as the prototype Sandringham 1. A new, elegant nose and tail replaced the Sunderland's converted turrets and the vastly improved interior had two decks, cocktail bar and a proper dining saloon. The Twin Wasp-powered Sandringham Mk.2, Mk.3, Mk.5 and Mk.7, all of which were conversions of Sunderland 5s, were externally similar to the unique Sandringham 1.

Sandringham sales included three 45-seater Mk.2s and two 21-seater Mk.3s bought by the Argentine operator Dodero. After Aerolineas Argentinas took over Dodero, their fleet was increased with the purchase of two Sunderland 5s. CAUSA of Uruguay and ALFA of Argentina each bought a Sunderland 3 which had been fitted with a Sandringham interior. In 1946, four 30-seat Sandringham 4s were delivered to the New Zealand airline, Tasman Empire Airways Ltd (TEAL) and in 1948, three 37-seat radar-equipped Sandringham 6s were sold to DNL Norway for their Oslo-Tromso service. BOAC bought nine 'Plymouth' Class Sandringham Mk.5s in 1947 followed in 1948 by the only three examples of the Mk.7 variant, known to them as the 'Bermuda' Class.

After the Sunderlands and Sandringhams were replaced by Constellations in BOAC service, three surviving Sandringham 5s were sold to Qantas, two Mk.7s went to CAUSA and the other Mk.7 was overhauled at Cowes by Saunders-Roe and delivered to Captain Sir Gordon Taylor. This aircraft, 'Frigate Bird', flew to Australia in 1954 to operate 'cruises' in the South Seas and in 1958 it was sold to RAI in Tahiti. This aircraft, F-OBIP, still exists in storage at the Musée de l'Air in Paris. The only other surviving Sandringham is VH-BRC at the Southampton Hall of Aviation.

The 34-seater Short S.45 Solent was slightly longer and much heavier than the

Sunderland/Sandringham. Powered by Bristol Hercules engines, it had a wider fuselage and a luxurious cabin complete with two decks containing a cocktail bar, a library and a promenade deck. 12 Solent 2s were delivered to BOAC in 1947/48 after the order for the RAF had cancelled the military Seaford version. BOAC also obtained six Mk.3s that had been converted to Solents during their construction at Belfast as Seaford 1s. On 10th November 1950, all BOAC flying boat services ceased. The Solents were then sold; four to Trans-Oceanic Airways in Sydney, Australia; one to TEAL, to join their four Solent 4s already in service; and another four to Hamble-based Aquila Airways for services to the Canaries and Madeira.

Surviving Solents are N9946F at the Western Aerospace Museum in Oakland, California and ZK-AMO which was retired by TEAL in 1960 and later preserved at the Museum of Transport and Technology in Auckland, New Zealand. In Polk City, Florida the world's last airworthy Shorts flying boat is Sunderland N814ML; in the 1980s, this had been UK-based as G-BJHS.

Specifications (for the Short Solent 2)

Span: 34.36m (112ft 9½in)
Length: 26.70m (87ft 8in)
Engines: Four 1260kW (1,690hp) Bristol
    Hercules 637 piston radials
Cruise speed: 393km/h (244mph)
Accommodation: 34

Many enthusiasts, myself included, took advantage of the opportunity to fly in this magnificent Short Sandringham VP-LVE in September 1976. Captained by the legendary Charles Blair, it operated a series of joy rides from Studland Bay around the Isle of Wight. (Author)

Note the enlarged tail fin and extra cabin windows on this Short Solent. Preserved for many years at the MOTAT Museum in Auckland, New Zealand, ZK-AMO flew TEAL's last flying boat service in September 1960. (Dave Howell collection)

I-DAXA was the first Series III Caravelle to be delivered to Alitalia in April 1960. The aircraft's name 'Altair' was the same as the Italian airline that operated a fleet of five Caravelles in the mid-1980s. (John Wegg collection)

SUD-EST SE-210 CARAVELLE
Société Nationale de Construction Aéronautique du Sud-Est, Toulouse
France

The excellent design of the Caravelle and its fine passenger comforts has ensured its place in any list of classic airliners. However, the current and future noise restrictions in Europe and North America have grounded this graceful transport in most of the world.

The Caravelle evolved from a French government requirement for a fast airliner which could link France with its dependent countries in northern Africa. Announced in 1953, the Caravelle showed significant improvements from previous French-built airliners. With the excellent Rolls-Royce Avon engines positioned on either side of the rear fuselage, a short undercarriage could be used. This permitted easy access to the cabin and the 'clean' wing, free from any engine attachments or wash from propellers gave excellent aerodynamic efficiency. One feature not so advanced, was the result of design assistance by de Havilland; the entire forward fuselage, including the cockpit, is an exact replica of the DH Comet including the cockpit windows. The only obvious differences were the two sets of engine controls and a two-crew cockpit. The Caravelle's unique triangular cabin window shape became symbolic of the type and was often used in advertising.

With the French Government providing financial help, two flying prototypes were assembled and successfully flown at Toulouse. Air France placed the first order for 12 Caravelles in February 1956.

Subsequent orders arrived in small numbers until Air France ordered 12 Series 3s in July 1958, but perhaps the most significant breakthrough occurred in 1960. At that time, only SAS, Air France and Varig were operating Caravelles, but the American sales tour made by the second prototype in Spring 1957 had interested United Airlines and they later placed an order for 20 of the proposed Series 6R in February 1960. However, this American love affair with the Caravelle was short-lived for within three years United and TWA were cancelling their options and orders and the adventurous sales and technical support agreement signed with Douglas in 1960 was embarrassingly dropped. No further airline sales were made in the USA.

Until the development of the Series 10B in the mid-1960s, all production Caravelles were powered by Rolls-Royce RA.29 Avon turbojets and had similar external dimensions. None of these Avon powered aircraft (Series 1, 1A, 3, 6N and 6R) are currently airworthy. The series 3 was the most popular Caravelle version with a total production run of 78.

First flown in March 1964, the Pratt & Whitney powered Caravelle 10B was a stretched (1.00m/3ft 3in) 109-seater which operated its first service for Finnair four months later. Only six examples of the 11R 'Combi' version, which had a large forward freight door and an APU, were built for Air Afrique, Air Congo and Transeuropa.

Twelve examples of the final Caravelle variant to be built were ordered by the Danish airline Sterling and French domestic operator Air Inter. The 140-seat stretched Series 12 was 36.24m (118ft 11in) long and had JT8D-9 engines. It first entered service with Sterling in March 1971 and the last one built was delivered to Air Inter in March 1973.

With no hush kit or new engine available, the type is now banned by many countries because of its unacceptable noise. In March 1999 about 75 Caravelles still survived including 11 airworthy examples in service in Colombia, the Democratic Republic of Congo and South Africa. Others have found new lives in museums or as cabin trainers, restaurants, instructional airframes and even as advertising hoardings. Many are scattered throughout France including the first production aircraft, used for ground instruction at Vilgenis near Paris. Others survive in Belgrade, Brussels, Billund, Cincinnati, Columbus, Cuba, Damascus, Denmark, Ecuador, Istanbul, Italy, Oslo, Thessaloniki, Tucson, Tunisia, Van Nuys and Windsor Locks.

Specifications (for the Series 10B)

Span: 34.30m (112ft 6in)
Length: 33.01m (108ft 3in)
Engines: Two 62.3kN (14,000lb)
   Pratt & Whitney JT8D-7 turbofans
Cruise speed: 825km/h (445kts) maximum
Accommodation: 100 maximum

Another shot from Gatwick's control tower shows one of Altair's Caravelle 10s in August 1984. I-GISI was originally delivered to Finnair and is currently believed to exist in Colombia. (Author)

Military Caravelles were operated in Argentina, France, Mexico, Sweden and Yugoslavia. This Series 11R was bought by the French Armée de l'Air second-hand in 1976 and is seen in current service as 9Q-CNA with Malu Aviation and named 'Lynn'. (African Aviation Slide Service)

This very early shot of Tu-104A CCCP-L5445 was taken at New York Idlewild airport in June 1956, a few months before the type officially entered commercial service. Note the LAV and TWA Constellations in the background. (Author's collection)

TUPOLEV Tu-104

Tupolev Joint Stock Company
15, Akademika Tupoleva, Moscow 111250
Russia

The Soviet Union's insistence on homegrown airliners for Aeroflot occasionally forced their manufacturers to take short cuts to satisfy the demands for aircraft comparable to the new Western offerings. Based on the design of a jet bomber, the swiftly produced Tu-104 was overpowered, thirsty for fuel and lacked a modern cabin, but it was reliable and strong and it became the Soviet Union's first passenger jet and Aeroflot's standard medium-range airliner. Aeroflot's Tu-104s had carried over 100 million passengers by the time the last one was retired in August 1981.

Under the leadership of A N Tupolev, design work on the Tu-104 commenced in 1953 alongside a jet bomber designated the Tu-16. In order to expedite the construction and development of the airliner, many Tu-16 assemblies were utilised in the building of the prototype Tu-104. Five prototypes were completed at Moscow-Bykovo using a brand new pressurised circular cross-section fuselage mated to Tu-16 wings, tail unit, nose, undercarriage and engines. In addition, a batch of at least half a dozen Tu-16s was converted to Tu-104G configuration. Main production commenced at Kharkov in 1956 and at Kazan in 1958.

The bomber's 35° leading edge sweep and the undercarriage's trailing-edge fairings became standard on Tupolev jet airliners including the Tu-124, 134 and 154. One item

which was also found on the Caravelle was the braking parachute. In the 1950s, the standard runway was designed to accept propeller transports, so the landing run of a large and fast jet such as the Tu-104, particularly in poor weather, could prove to be a problem. The Tu-104's twin braking parachutes were essential in such circumstances, and I can well remember seeing the havoc caused at Gatwick if the Aeroflot captain dropped his parachutes on the runway rather than on the taxiway!

The prototype Tu-104 first flew on 17th June 1955, and the type entered service on the Moscow-Omsk-Irkutsk route on 15th September 1956. Prior to this, the prototype Tu-104 created a great deal of interest for western journalists when it brought General Serov to London Heathrow in March 1956.

Approximately 207 new-build Tu-104s were manufactured. The 'A' version, compared to the original 104, had a revised 70-seater cabin and entered Aeroflot service in 1957. Ninety-seven 100-seater Tu-104Bs were built with a 1.21m (3ft 11½in) fuselage stretch and several Tu-104As were converted to 100-seaters, without the stretch, and given the designation Tu-104V. The Czechoslovakian airline CSA made the only export order for the Tu-104 when it bought six Tu-104A for its medium range services.

A couple of Tu-104s were modified at the factory as 78-100 seater four-engined Tu-110s.

First flown in 1957 and displayed at Moscow in July that year, the Tu-110 had excellent performance but was rejected by Aeroflot and ended its days with the Soviet Air Force.

Aeroflot continued to operate Tu-104s until the type was retired in August 1981. Since then most aircraft have been scrapped but several still exist in museums and elsewhere. One ex-CSA Tu-104A is preserved at the Kbely museum near Prague while two others are currently in use as restaurants at Olomouc and Petrovice. A fourth ex-CSA Tu-104A is dumped near Nicosia airport in Cyprus. Approximately ten ex-Aeroflot and Soviet Air Force Tu-104s are preserved in the FSU; a few of them are in use at training institutes while others just rot where they were dumped. In 1976, to celebrate 20 years of passenger jet aviation, an Aeroflot Tu-104 was ceremonially preserved on the 'Pedestal of Glory' at Vnukovo Airport, Moscow.

Specifications (for the Tu-104B)

Span: 34.54m (113ft 4in)
Length: 40.06m (131ft 5in)
Engines: Two 9700kg (21,384lb) thrust
    Mikulin RD-3M-500 turbojets
Cruise speed: 800 km/h (497 mph)
Accommodation: 100

This immaculate Aeroflot Tu-104B was built at Kazan around 1960 and was photographed at London Heathrow in September 1970. It later crashed on take-off at Moscow-Sheremetyevo on 28th November 1976. (Paul Huxford)

Still retaining its elegance despite the ravages of time, Tu-104B CCCP-42441 managed to beat the scrap men by becoming a training airframe at the Aviation Institute at Samara-Uchebny. (Author's collection)

As can be seen by the amount of attendant vehicles, the arrival of one of these giants at Heathrow always created a stir. This Tu-114B CCCP-76485 was photographed in July 1966, and 35 years later it still exists at Krivoy Reg. (Author's collection)

TUPOLEV Tu-114 'ROSSIYA'

Tupolev Joint Stock Company
15, Akademika Tupoleva
Moscow 111250, Russia

Developed from the famous Tu-20 (Tu-95) bomber known in the west as the 'Bear', this incredible airliner reportedly made its first flight on 3rd November 1957. In 1959, it was the star at the Paris Air Show and later made two flights to New York. These 11-hour non-stop flights by the prototype culminated in the Soviet Premier, Mr Khruschev, flying in one to New York on 15th September 1959 and to Andrews Air Force Base, Washington on 15th October. After many months of long-range route proving trials, the Tu-114 entered non-stop commercial service on the 8½ hour Moscow to Khabarovsk route in April 1961. The type's first visit to the UK was in February 1963, when one collected 170 British newspaper businessmen from Heathrow and took them to Moscow for a goodwill visit.

The first regular weekly non-stop service from Moscow to Havana commenced on 7th January 1963. The Tu-114s operated flight SU-047 with a reduced capacity for only 60 passengers in a planned time of 20 hours 5 minutes. With the favourable westerly winds, the returning SU-048 to Moscow took 'only' 16 hours 25 minutes! My 1963 Aeroflot timetable also shows a Tu-114 departing from Moscow (Sheremetyevo) to Delhi every Monday. The high speed of the 'Rossiya' is demonstrated by the quoted flight time of 6 hours 35 minutes, exactly the same as the Air India Boeing 707. These very long flights were later amended with stops at Conakry on the

Cuba run, and at Tashkent on the trip to Delhi. In 1965, Aeroflot and Japan Air Lines began discussions for a joint non-stop service between Moscow and Tokyo. This commenced in April 1967 using two dedicated Tu-114s carrying extra Japan Air Lines titles on the fuselage. Other Tu-114 destinations included Accra, Algiers, Murmansk, Paris and Montreal.

A total of 33 Tu-114s were built at Samara in Russia, and as well as being the world's fastest propeller-driven transport, the Tu-114 (NATO code name 'Cleat') was also the world's largest airliner until overtaken by the Boeing 747. The eight cabins with six-abreast seating normally accommodated 150; however it was also reported using high-density 220-passenger eight-abreast seating for routes to Alma-Ata and Sukhumi. Notable features were the very long nosewheel leg, the highly swept anhedral wing, the huge Kuznetsov turboprop engines and the giant 5.60m (18ft 4½ in) diameter four-blade contra-rotating propellers. The height of the fuselage from the ground, at 5m (16ft), could cause a few problems with ground equipment. On the type's first visit to Heathrow, an extra set of steps had to be placed on top of the normal ones to reach the cabin!

Mention must be made of the Tu-116 which first flew in 1957. Two civilian examples of this special long-range version of the Tu-114 were built using converted Tu-20 bomber

fuselages. The narrow cabin was pressurised only in the rear with seats for 30 passengers and it seems they were used as high-speed long-range transports for VIPs; indeed it is rumoured that they were there for the leaders' escape to Cuba or wherever if things should all go pear-shaped! Remarkably, one of these aircraft, also known to Aeroflot as the Tu-114D, still exists at the Museum of Civil Aviation, Ulyanovsk.

When the type was finally withdrawn from service in 1977, a few of the survivors were donated to technical schools and museums. To mark the Tu-114's significant contribution to Soviet aviation, one example was restored in the late 1970s and ceremonially preserved on a massive plinth outside Moscow Domodedovo airport. About seven more Tu-114s are currently 'preserved' at Monino, Novgorod, Moscow and Ulyanovsk. In 1999 a Tu-114B was discovered at a technical school at Krivoy Rog in the Ukraine; it had flown into the grass strip there in 1978.

Specifications

Span: 51.00m (167ft 4in)
Length: 54.00m (177ft 2in)
Engines: Four 11,033kW (14,795hp)
  Kuznetsov NK-12M turboprops
Cruise speed: 800km/h (497mph)
Accommodation: Normally 150/170, max 220

Tupolev Tu-114B CCCP-76464 was photographed at Paris-Le Bourget in September 1966. In 1967 it was the first Tu-114 to be jointly operated by Japan Air Lines and Aeroflot between Moscow and Tokyo. This aircraft is currently preserved at Domodedovo. (Author's collection)

Photographed at the Monino Museum in 1991, CCCP-L5611 is a Tu-114A which first flew in November 1957. Note the revised colour scheme and the Lisunov Li-2 and Antonov An-22 behind. (Author's collection)

Taken at Heathrow in June 1970, this picture shows OK-TEA, the first of three Tu-124Vs bought by CSA. The crest by the rear door carries the name 'Melnik'. This aircraft was withdrawn by CSA in 1972 and later sold to Iraq. (Author's collection)

TUPOLEV Tu-124

Tupolev Joint Stock Company
15, Akademika Tupoleva, Moscow 111250
Russia

Looking at this sleek jetliner, one would be surprised to know that is was planned as a replacement for the piston-engined Ilyushin IL-14 (see page 106) on the short domestic Aeroflot schedules radiating from the airports of Moscow. Reportedly, the air-passenger populations of most of the cities within one hour's flying of Moscow were not large enough to justify using the Tu-104 or IL-18, so Tupolev was tasked with producing the USSR's first short-haul jetliner.

Because the new airliner needed to be able to operate from relatively short runways, great attention was paid to providing a good short-field performance and a strong undercarriage. Using their Tu-104 medium-range airliner (see page 138) as a basis, Tupolev designers shortened the fuselage to accommodate 44 seats and completely redesigned the wings. The new Tu-124 had rearward extensions to the wing section between the engines and the fairings housing the undercarriage and double slotted trailing edge flaps. In order to provide assistance to the braking when operating into short runways, the crew could deploy the tail braking parachute which was featured on the Tu-104, but this was seldom necessary because of the advanced system of wing-mounted automatic lift-dumpers. During a landing these devices emerged from the top of the wing as soon as the weight of the aircraft was on the main landing gear. In flight, they could be manually operated and used as

spoilers to reduce air speed. Further modifications included a quick-retracting short-stroke undercarriage and a large ventral air brake which was deployed on approach to steepen the glide angle and to provide additional runway braking.

Perhaps the Tu-124s greatest advancement over the Tu-104 was the introduction of the new turbofan engines. The Soloviev D-20P engines were significantly quieter than the Tu-104's smoky Mikulin turbojets and more importantly, they were far more fuel-efficient.

The prototype Tu-124 first flew on 24th March 1960 and following successful trials, the type entered production at GAZ number 135 at Kharkov. First commercial service with Aeroflot was from Moscow to Tallinn (Estonia) on 2nd October 1962 followed by Moscow to Ulyanovsk on 10th November. Not only was the Tu-124 the first Soviet-built turbofan-powered airliner to enter scheduled service, it also beat its western equivalents, the BAC 1-11 and DC-9 into service by nearly two years.

The 56-seater Tu-124V was the first variant to appear and this became the most widely used in service. Three Tu-124Vs were ordered by CSA in Czechoslovakia and two by Interflug in East Germany. In 1966, the Indian Air Force received three examples of the executive 36-seater Tu-124K for use by their high-ranking officers and politicians. An even more deluxe interior was provided in the

Tu-124K2 version that had only 22 seats.

112 Tu-124s (Nato reporting name 'Cookpot') were built; most of them were delivered to Aeroflot, but a few did operate with the Soviet, Iraqi, Chinese and East German Air Forces. The two CSA aircraft were sold to Iraqi Airways in 1973 and Aeroflot ceased all services with their Tu-124s on 21st January 1980. The Tu-134 design was based on the Tu-124 and it is reported that a couple of dismantled 124s were used in the construction of the prototype Tu-134s.

Three Tu-124s survive outside the FSU. In China, the Datang Shan Museum has two ex-Chinese Air Force examples on display, one of which has been dramatically painted in an odd colour scheme and the Indian Air Force museum maintains one of their retired Tu-124Ks. A surprising number of Tu-124s are reported to survive in the FSU; the easiest to find is probably the one at Monino but others are preserved/stored/dumped at Astrakhan, Grondo, Kharkov North, Kuadorovsk, Kubinka, Mineralnye Vody, Novosibirsk, Omsk, Savelovo and Ulyanovsk.

Specifications

Span: 25.55m (83ft 9¼in)
Length: 30.58m (100ft 4in)
Engines: Two 5,400kg (11,905lb) Soloviev D-20P turbofans
Cruise speed: 770 km/h (480mph)
Accommodation: 50

Despite it carrying full Aeroflot colours, this Tupolev Tu-124 was reportedly flown on behalf of the Soviet Air Force when photographed at Helsinki in June 1980. (Author's collection)

One of the three Tu-124Ks delivered to the Indian Air Force in 1966 has been preserved at the IAF Museum at Palam in New Delhi. V644 'Rajdoot' is seen here in October 1997 alongside a C-119, an IL-14 and an An-12. (Simon Watson)

Note the beautiful old colour scheme on this early series Tu-134 at Heathrow in April 1969. Built at Kharkov in 1967, it survived many years of service before it was broken up at St. Petersburg in 1991. (Colin Ballantine collection)

TUPOLEV Tu-134

Tupolev Joint Stock Company
15, Akademika Tupoleva, Moscow 111250
Russia

After Soviet Premier Nikita Khrushchev had flown in a Caravelle, he reportedly instructed Tupolev to begin work on a new airliner with rear-mounted engines which could emulate the cabin quietness of this new western-built jetliner. Three years later the Tu-134 was flown and despite its shortcomings of high fuel consumption and relatively poor performance, the type proved to be a success, becoming the standard short/medium range jet airliner in the Soviet Union and in Eastern Europe. A very respectable total of 853 were built between 1963 and 1984 with the majority of the 170 exports going to the East European airlines including Balkan Bulgarian, CSA, Interflug and Malev.

Having used the Tu-16 as a basis for the Tu-104, and that as a basis for the Tu-124, Tupolev's team went another step further with the basic design to produce an airliner with rear-mounted engines, a new wing and a 'T' tail. The all new wing was longer than the 124's and, like its predecessors, carried Tupolev's trademark fairings housing the retracted main undercarriage. The 104/124 fuselage cross section was retained and the basic 124 fuselage was stretched by 0.66m (2ft 2in); the nose section retained the glazed navigator's position and the weather radar under the cockpit floor, while an obvious difference was additional cockpit windows.

As the design developed further and further from the Tu-124, the original designation of

Tu-124A was changed to Tu-134 in 1963. The components for the two prototype Tu-134s were manufactured at Kharkov. These were then transported to the Tupolev factory in the centre of Moscow for assembly and investigation prior to their disassembly for transport to the Zhukovsky test facility where they were once again reassembled. The prototype made its first flight there as the 'Tu-134-1' on 29th July 1963. Like the British-built 'T' tailed BAC1-11, the Tu-134 development aircraft suffered 'deep stall' problems leading to the crash of one of the prototypes. Increasing the size of the tailplane rectified the problem and the type was revealed to the public in September 1964. Its western debut was at the Paris Air Show in 1965 and in August 1967 a production model Tu-134 (NATO reporting name 'Crusty') flew the first Aeroflot passenger service from Moscow to Belgrade.

An improved version, the 80-seater Tu-134A first flew in 1969 and began Aeroflot services in 1970. This had a 2.7m (8ft 8in) fuselage stretch, and various improvements including more efficient Soloviev D-30-2 turbofans with thrust reversers, strengthened undercarriage, new radios, brakes, wheels, navigation equipment and an APU. This version became the standard production model for many years and achieved dozens of foreign sales including several for military use.

The further updated model Tu-134B first appeared in 1980. This dispensed with the

navigator's position behind the somewhat sinister 'bomb-aimer' glass nose and moved it to a more conventional position in the cockpit. The weather radar was then repositioned to the nose cone. Apart from Aeroflot use, the Tu-134B was exported to Bulgaria, Vietnam, Syria and North Korea.

Further variants included the Tu-134A1/Tu-134A2 followed by the Tu-134A3 and the 96-seater B3 both with more efficient Soloviev D-30-III engines. Several military and 'one-off' conversions include the Tu-160 crews, the Tu-134BSh nav trainer, the Tu-135 with stinger tail, the Tu-134SKh crop surveyor, the Tu-134BV for space shuttle work and the Tu-134LK cosmonaut trainer.

Tu-134A and B models were delivered new to 13 different countries, but surprisingly none were sold in China. Production ceased in 1985, and of the 853 built, possibly 400 are still active, mostly in the FSU. The largest fleets are currently with Air Kharkov, Air Ukraine, Komiinteravia, Pulkovo Airlines, Tyumen Airlines and Voronezhavia, while elsewhere, Syrianair and Air Koryo are still believed to have a few Tu-134s.

Specifications (for the Tu-134A)

Span: 29.00m (95ft 2in)
Length: 37.10m (121ft 9in)
Engines: Two 66.7kN (14,990lb)
Soloviev D-30-2 turbofans
Cruise speed: 820km/h (443kts)
Accommodation: 76

Tu-134A YU-AHX was delivered new to Aviogenex in March 1971. Seen here at Gatwick in 1985, it was later returned to the Soviet Union prior to re-sale to Aero Tumi in Peru. It was last known with Imperial Air at Lima in 1994. (Author)

St. Petersburg-based Pulkovo Air Enterprise's Tu-134A-3 RA-65004 blasts off from runway 26L at Gatwick in April 1998 operating Aeroflot Russian International's flight AFL661. Pulkovo have eleven Tu-134s in their fleet. (Author)

Note the lack of forward fuselage canards and the different tailfin profile on the prototype Tu-144 compared to later versions. Carrying a special registration to indicate the year of production, it was seen during its first ever visit to the West at the 1971 Paris Air Show. (Harry Holmes)

TUPOLEV Tu-144

Tupolev Joint Stock Company
15, Akademika Tupoleva, Moscow 111250
Russia

In addition to the space race between the Russian and American space agencies, the Russian aircraft industry was also keen to show the world that they could compete with the West when it came to advanced passenger airliners. The Tupolev design bureau first proposed their concept of a supersonic passenger airliner in the early 1960s. By 1965 the layout was defined enough for Tupolev to display models of their radical new airliner, the Tu-144, at the Paris Air Salon. Just as the Concorde wing design was tested using the BAC Type 221 experimental aircraft, so the Russians tested and refined their supersonic wing layout using a MiG-21 fighter aircraft fitted with a scaled-down version of the Tu-144's wing.

Two months ahead of Concorde, the prototype Tu-144 (CCCP-68001) became the world's first supersonic airliner to fly when Captain Eduard V Yelian took-off from Zhukovsky on 31st December 1968; unusually for a prototype civil airliner, both pilots were given ejection seats. Embarrassed at being beaten by the Soviets, Concorde's British and French manufacturers moaned that they had cut corners and had resorted to espionage in an effort to rush the Tu-144 into the air before the Anglo-French airliner. However, both aircraft were developed independently and despite their external similarities, they were very different. The Tu-144 had a much simpler wing than

Concorde and used a significant amount of titanium structures to withstand the heat and expansion caused by high-speed friction. The prototype also had its four 17,500kg (38,580lb) Kuznetsov engines mounted in a single underwing fairing, unlike the two dual pods on the Concorde.

It was the designed cruise speed of the Tu-144 and Concorde that dictated their similar shape, and the problem of reduced forward visibility caused by the high angle of attack on take-off/landing was solved by both manufacturers adopting a complicated and expensive drooping nose. The Russians charmingly called theirs a 'pecking' nose.

The Tu-144 prototype was followed by 12 extensively modified models which were 6.00m (19ft 7in) longer. These production aircraft had more powerful NK-144 engines arranged in podded pairs similar to Concorde and had small retractable 'canard' wings fitted behind the cockpit to improve low speed control. The main undercarriage was also simplified by replacing the prototype's 12-wheel main bogies with an 8-wheel version. It was one of these aircraft that suffered a tragic and controversial crash whilst demonstrating at Paris in June 1973.

Aeroflot struggled to introduce the Tu-144 into regular service. Fuel consumption was high, the cabin was very noisy and the sonic boom was an environmental problem, but regular freight/mail services began on 26th

December 1975 between Moscow and Almaty followed by the first passenger service on the same route in November 1977. The awful economics of the type together with a fatal crash in May 1978 led the authorities to suspend all flights the following month.

At least five examples of the heavier (190,000kg/419,000lb MTOW) Tu-144D were built. These had greater fuel capacity and range, but as they were completed after 1978, they did very little flying. Recently, a Tu-144D was re-activated for use by NASA as a supersonic testbed. The refurbished Tu-144LL was given new engines and avionics and first flew at Zhukovsky on 29th October 1996 prior to commencing a series of 19 flights, funded by NASA, to assist a US development programme for a second generation SST. The last of these test flights was flown in February 1998.

Several surviving examples can be found in Russia. The museums at Monino and Ulyanovsk each have one on display and others can found in storage particularly at Zhukovsky where the Tu-144LL and one other are still believed to be airworthy.

Specifications (for the Tu-144)

Span: 28.80m (94ft 5½ in)
Length: 65.70m (215ft 6½ in)
Engines: Four 20,000kg (44,092lb)
    Kuznetsov NK-144 turbofans
Cruise speed: 2,300km/h (1,429 mph)
Accommodation: 60-70, maximum 140

Towering above the massed crowds and metal barriers that cause such aggravation to aircraft photographers at air shows, this Tu-144 also has a contrived registration. CCCP-77144 was displayed at the 1975 Paris Show. (Author's collection)

This Tu-144 was retired in 1981 with total of 314 airframe hours and 212 landings. It is currently preserved at the Museum of Civil Aviation in Ulyanovsk, still showing its Paris display number. (Frank Tornow)

The second VFW 614 built, D-BABB, was first flown in January 1972. Seen here in company colours, it displays the flag of its home town Bremen on the fuselage. (Author's collection)

VFW-FOKKER VFW 614

VFW-Fokker GmbH
Bremen
Germany

Unfortunately for this relatively unknown, but perfectly serviceable short-haul airliner, the positioning of its engines on pylons above the wings caused it to become the butt of many jokes. Derided as having its wings on upside down, the VFW 614 caused a few smiles wherever it went. Whether these jibes affected sales is not known, but what is known is that despite a market estimate of 350-400 aircraft, only 19 were completed and the type became a financial disaster for the companies involved.

Initial development work of the 614 by Fokker and VFW (Vereinigte Flugtechnische Werke GmbH) commenced in 1963 after the Federal German Government had agreed to provide financial backing for the construction and development of three prototypes. The programme was designed as a collaborative venture under the leadership of VFW-Fokker but with participation in the production and development from MBB in Germany and SABCA and Fairey in Belgium. The VFW 614 was the first passenger jetliner to enter 'large' scale production in West Germany.

Construction of the first aircraft started in August 1968 and at the time of the successful first flight on 14th July 1971, the type had attracted several unconfirmed orders from airlines around the world. The airlines who were prepared to reveal their interest were Bavaria Fluggesellschaft, Cimber Air, Filipinas Orient, General Air, Sterling Airways and Yemen Airlines. Other options were obtained

from the Spanish Ministry of Aviation and the Société de Travail Aérien.

In 1969, Fokker and VFW became equal partners in Fokker-VFW and both companies became heavily involved in the highly complex VAK 191B experimental V/STOL strike/ reconnaissance aircraft. In a tragedy which disrupted pre-certification test flying and probably damaged sales prospects, the first prototype VFW 614 was destroyed in a crash near Bremen while on a routine test flight in February 1972. After the crash, major modifications were made to the elevator control system and no further handling problems were encountered. Indeed, the other aircraft flew very well and because the engines were positioned near to the centre-line of the aircraft, there was no change to the pitch when the throttles were moved either way. Other advantages gained from the engine positioning were a reduction in foreign object ingestion, greater flap area due to the lack of a cut-out in the wing, quieter noise 'footprint' on the ground and a short landing gear allowing the use of a simple air stair behind the door.

Despite the setback of the accident, construction of the first batch of ten production aircraft commenced in April 1973, by which time most of the orders had disappeared. From the original list of potential customers, only Cimber Air maintained a continued interest, but new orders had been gained from the French airlines Touraine Air

Transport and Air Alsace. The first production aircraft was flown on 28th April 1975 and delivered to Cimber Air four months later. Plans for the licence production of the 614 in Romania and the production of a stretched 60-seater GAC-616 to be built by Gulfstream American Corp came to nought. By the end of 1977 it was obvious that no further orders would be obtained and VFW-Fokker closed down the Bremen production line.

Currently, two VFW 614s are active. One is owned and operated by the German research company DLR Flugbetriebe (Deutsches Zentrum fur Luft und Raumfahrt) based at Oberpfaffenhofen. Since December 1994 this aircraft has been employed on the examination and analysis of jet aircraft exhaust emissions in flight. The unique positioning of the engines has proved ideal for this research because the exhaust emissions can be observed from inside the cabin. The other is based at Bremen as an 'ATD' (Advanced Technology Demonstrator). Three VIP VFW 614s retired by the German Air Force in 1998 may possibly find homes in civilian life as they have now been registered in Denmark.

Specifications

Span: 21.50m (70ft 6½in)
Length: 20.60m (67ft 7in)
Engines: Two 33.8kN (7,600lb)
   Rolls-Royce SNECMA M45H turbofans
Cruise speed: 722 km/h (390kts) maximum
Accommodation: 40, maximum 44

Still with its German registration on 23rd May 1976, D-BABE shortly became F-GATG with Air Alsace. This aircraft was eventually scrapped at Lemwerder in November 1980. (Author's collection)

Delivered new to the West German Air Force in May 1977, VIP transport VFW 614 17+01 was finally retired on March 31st 1998. Three WGAF VFW 614s, including this one, have been re-registered in Denmark and flown to Sweden to await a new career. (Author's collection)

This remarkable aircraft was once the world's first pure jet transport! In 1947 it was converted to take two Rolls-Royce Nene turbojets in place of the Hercules engines. The Nene Viking was converted back to a Viking 1B and bought by Eagle in 1953. (Tony Eastwood collection)

VICKERS VIKING

Vickers-Armstrongs Ltd
Brooklands and Wisley Aerodromes, Surrey
England

Unlike the major American aircraft manufacturers, the British had, of necessity, concentrated mostly on fighters and bombers during the Second World War. Apart from the Avro York, very little was done that would produce a new British-built airliner for service immediately after the war. The new types recommended by the Brabazon committee would not be ready soon enough: the need was for an interim type that could be built quickly and cheaply to supplement and improve on the DC-3.

Vickers' designers studied three civil developments of current Vickers bombers and chose the 'Wellington Continental' in preference to airliners based on the Warwick or the Windsor. By utilising many Wellington assemblies, the new airliner, to be known as the VC.1 (Vickers Commercial One), could be developed without delay. A brand new stressed-skin metal fuselage was designed after the original proposal for a fabric covered one was rejected as being too difficult to maintain. Wellington components used were the geodetically constructed fabric-covered outer wings and tailplanes and the nacelles; a modified and improved Wellington/Warwick tailwheel undercarriage and the Mark X Wellington's Bristol Hercules engine.

Given the name previously used on their 1919 amphibian, the prototype Viking first flew at Wisley on 22nd June 1945. Nineteen Type 498 Vikings were ordered by BOAC for their European services. Some of these were

sent to the West Indies and others were used for military trials leaving only 11 (later designated Mk.1As) to be operated by BEA after BOAC had been reorganised.

In 1946, the first 'long-nose' 24-passenger Mk.1B with a 0.71m (2ft 4in) fuselage stretch was revealed. This had the all-new metal wing and tailplane demanded by BEA for their 13 Type 614 Viking Mk.1s. Foreign orders were obtained from Aer Lingus, BWIA, Central African, DDL (Denmark), Indian National, Iraqi, South African and Suidair International.

In total, 163 Vikings were built between 1945 and 1949 and although it had a reasonable safety record, its poor de-icing equipment and its tendency to tip on its nose when landing empty caused several incidents. During the mid to late 1950s, the Vikings were replaced in front-line service by turboprop types but many found new careers with the independent airlines operating the new inclusive tours in Europe. Fitted with 32 seats, large numbers were bought and operated by West German charter airlines and UK airlines including Air Ferry, Air Safaris, Autair, BKS, Continental, Channel, Overseas and Tradair.

The modified military version of the Viking, the Valetta, was first flown in June 1947. 263 Valettas (C.1, C.2, T.3 and T.4) provided impeccable service to the RAF in a huge variety of roles including troop carrier, nav trainer, freighter, ambulance, glider tug and VIP and paratroop transport. Only two Valettas

survive; one is preserved at the Cosford Aerospace Museum and the other is at Flixton in Suffolk. The upgraded and larger Varsity, with a tricycle-undercarriage and belly pannier, was used by the RAF for twin-engined training, navigation and bomb-aiming instruction. First flown in July 1949, 163 were built, but none saw use as airliners.

Most Vikings had been scrapped by 1965; however, a few did soldier on with operators like Air Ferry, Autair and Invicta until 1969. Currently there are six Vikings preserved including two military examples in Argentina and Pakistan. Brooklands Museum is currently restoring the oldest surviving example G-AGRU; the SAA Museum is restoring ZS-DKH (once famous for being mounted above 'Vic's Viking Garage' in Johannesburg) and G-AGRW is preserved by 'Flugzeug Oldies' in Vienna. In 1999, the crumbling remains of G-AIVG at the Musée National de l'Automobile in Mulhouse, France (often called the Schlumpf Museum) were offered for disposal. This severely corroded airframe may well supply bits and pieces for the refurbishment of G-AGRU at Brooklands.

Specifications (for the Viking 1B)

Span: 27.20m (89ft 3in)
Length: 19.86m (65ft 2in)
Engines: Two 1260kW (1,690hp)
　　Bristol Hercules 634 radial pistons
Cruise speed: 338km/h (210mph)
Accommodation: 24 (later 32)

Viking 1B G-AIVF had just been withdrawn from use by Manston-based Invicta when it was photographed there in February 1969. Previous operators included BEA and Balair of Switzerland. (Author's collection)

Not all rare and interesting airliners manage to survive. This beautiful 1946-vintage Viking 1 G-AHPB looked fantastic at Düsseldorf in 1987 but after a few years display at a museum in Switzerland, it was tragically broken up around 1992. (Author)

Bought from BEA by Lao Airlines in 1969, this short-lived colour scheme on G-APKF was changed before it was delivered as XW-TDN. The aircraft crashed in Cambodia in 1975. (Bernard King collection)

VICKERS VISCOUNT

British Aircraft Corporation Ltd
Brooklands Aerodrome, Byfleet Surrey
also at Hurn Airport, Bournemouth, England

The Viscount design evolved from discussions in 1944 between the Brabazon Committee and Vickers-Armstrong (Aircraft) Ltd. In March 1946, the British government ordered two prototypes of the proposed aircraft, originally christened 'Viceroy'. The prototype Viscount, G-AHRF, made its first flight from the grass runway at Wisley in July 1948. By 1950, the early 32-seater design had grown to accommodate 40 to 53 passengers, and was fitted with the latest RR Dart R.Da.3 engines. These improvements prompted BEA to order a large fleet of Viscount 701s. Subsequently, large numbers were ordered by airlines worldwide, even from aréas that were considered 'difficult' for British makers, such as the USA.

Over 70 different models were built and each customer was given a 'type number' which remained with the aircraft until it was either converted or scrapped. For instance, the first production version for BEA was the V.701, and the last Viscounts built for the Chinese airline CAAC in 1964, were V.843s.

The basic models include the original 700 Series and the heavier 700D with Dart R.Da.6s and multiple modifications to satisfy the American FAA requirements. All the Series 700s can be differentiated from the later Series 800 by their oval doors. The stretched 800 Series first appeared in July 1956 and the Series 810, first ordered by Continental Airlines in December 1955, introduced many refinements including the R.Da.7 engine and

some major structural strengthening.

Despite much optimism that the Viscount would still be flying in the UK in the year 2000, the type has now disappeared from the British skies. The last handful of flyable Viscounts was operated by British World Airlines from Southend in Essex. These have now been retired and in the summer of 1999, the last two airworthy Viscounts in the UK were checked over, refuelled and flown off to a new life in Africa. Despite the sad fact of their withdrawal in the UK, there is every chance that a Viscount in southern Africa will still be in airline service in the year 2000; fifty years after the type made history as the world's first turbine-powered airliner to fly a scheduled passenger service.

As they are the only operator of an airworthy preserved Viscount, credit should be given to the Mid-Atlantic Air Museum in Reading, Pennsylvania. They maintain and fly N7471, a Viscount 789D which was operated for many years by a variety of corporate concerns in the USA. The aircraft is restored in magnificent red and white Capital Airlines colours and is flown to air shows in the USA. Apart from this airworthy example, very few Viscounts are currently operated on commercial services. The Democratic Republic of Congo, Gabon and South Africa have all had companies with Viscounts in their fleet in the last few years, but their continuing survival and long term prospects must be questionable.

Large numbers of preserved, stored and dumped Viscounts exist in the UK, of which the most famous preserved examples are G-ALWF and G-APIM. 'Whiskey Foxtrot' is the world's oldest Viscount (number 5) and is displayed in BEA colours amongst the amazing collection of British-built airliners at Duxford. 'India Mike', preserved at Brooklands Museum in Surrey, has a special meaning to me because it is named after the late Stephen Piercey who, apart from being a good friend, was the founding editor of 'Propliner' magazine and a fount of knowledge on all classic propeller airliners. I have the privilege to assist a team of 'Friends' who raise funds to maintain G-APIM in good condition.

Elsewhere in the world, various airlines, airports and museums have preserved examples of this historic and much-loved airliner. Non-flying Viscounts can be found in China, Brazil, Uruguay, France, Germany, Canada, Indonesia, Turkey and Zimbabwe.

Specifications

Span: Series 700D+810 28.56m(93ft 8in)
Length: Series 700D 24.91m(81ft 10in)
  Series 810 26.11m(85ft 8in)
Engines: Series 700D Four 1,193kW(1,600shp)
  RR Dart 510.
  Series 810 Four 1,566kW(2,100shp)
  RR Dart 541 turboprops
Cruise speed: 700D - 534km/h (290kts)
  810 - 640km/h (348kts)
Accommodation: 700D - 63. 810 - 75

A day never forgotten was when I accompanied Gordon Bain in a Piper Aztec from Southend in 1986 to capture Guernsey Airlines' immaculate Viscount 806 G-BLOA on film for use by BAF's publicity department. (Author)

A survivor from the British Air Ferries/British World Airlines fleet of Viscounts is this Series 806 G-APEY. Originally delivered to BEA in 1958, this aircraft now resides in the Gabon and retains its BAF colours. (African Aviation Slide Service)

This interesting night exposure was taken at Heathrow airport in 1965. V.953 Vanguard G-APEK was converted to Merchantman configuration in 1970 and was sold to Air Bridge Carriers by British Airways in November 1979. (Rolls-Royce)

VICKERS VANGUARD & MERCHANTMAN

Vickers Aviation,
Brooklands Aerodrome
Surrey, England

Encouraged by British European Airways who required a large, economical airliner for high density routes in Europe, and by Trans-Canada Air Lines who wanted a transcontinental 60-seater, the Vickers company started work on a suitable design in 1953. The differing requirements from each airline caused some design headaches, especially as BEA initially wanted a high-wing layout for passenger appeal, whilst TCA preferred conventional low-mounted wings! Turbojet power was considered, as were swept wings, high wings and dozens of alternative layouts, but by 1955 a conventional low wing layout with a 'double-bubble' fuselage was at last finding support from both of the airlines.

BEA ordered 20 of the Vickers Type 951 in July 1956, and in January 1957, TCA ordered 20 of the Type 952 which had a stronger airframe and higher gross weights and payload. The Type 953, offered to BEA in 1958, had better economics because of its greater maximum take-off weight. BEA thus changed their order to 6 V.951s and 14 V.953s.

The prototype Type 950, given the name 'Vanguard' by BEA, first flew from Brooklands on 20th January 1959 with the original fin lacking a dorsal fillet. Obvious similarities to its smaller brother, the Viscount, included identical cabin windows and the pronounced dihedral on the tailplane. The first Type 951 was delivered to BEA at Heathrow on 2nd December 1960 and the Vanguard

commenced official scheduled services by flying London to Paris on 1st March 1961.

With airlines clamouring for the latest jet airliners, Vanguard sales were disappointing. Only 44 Vanguards were built, but the type proved to be safe, reliable and economic for many years. The last BEA passenger Vanguard service was in June 1974, by which time several airframes had been converted to 'Merchantman' freighter configuration.

In 1966, an Air Canada Vanguard (cruelly nicknamed Mudguard in Canadian service!) was converted to an all-freight V.952F Cargoliner. This involved the removal of all passenger equipment and the blanking of the windows; however the standard passenger-door arrangement was retained. Its main duties were delivering mail to coastal regions and bringing back fresh lobsters. Similarly in 1968, BEA also decided to modify a number of Vanguards to an all-freight configuration. Renamed the Vickers V.953C 'Merchantman', the first one was converted by Aviation Traders Engineering Ltd (ATEL) at Southend and first flew on 10th October 1969. ATEL converted one other before BEA took over the work and converted seven more using kits supplied by ATEL. The modifications involved the removal of all passenger equipment and windows, strengthening the floor, fitting a mechanised cargo handling system and installing a 2.03m x 3.53m (6ft 8in x 11ft 7in) hydraulically operated forward cargo door.

After retirement from British Airways and Air Canada, most surviving Vanguards/Merchantmen found new careers. Most of the Canadian machines were bought by Air Holdings who leased or sold them to operators including Air Trader, Air Viking, Angkasa CAT, Europe Aero Service, Invicta International and Thor Cargo. Merpati Nusantara obtained 8 Vanguards for services in Indonesia and operated the last Vanguard passenger service in October 1987.

After replacement by a Lockheed Electra, Merchantman G-APEP became the last of the breed to fly on 17th October 1996. Hunting Cargo's Captain Peter Moore and co-pilot Gary West flew G-APEP back to her birthplace at Weybridge. The Vanguard, often referred to as the first 'Airbus', will not fly again; however 'Echo Papa' is kept in fine condition at the Brooklands Museum next to the VC-10 and the engines are run regularly. Unless there is still some remnants of a Vanguard at Perpignan in France, then the only other bits left are the nose of G-APEJ at Brooklands and the nose of G-APES at East Midlands airport.

Specifications (for the Type 953)

Span: 36.15m (118ft 7in)
Length: 37.45m (122ft 10½in)
Engines: Four 3,765kW (5,050shp)
Rolls-Royce Tyne RTy1 Mk.512
Cruise speed: 627 km/h (390mph)
Accommodation: 139
Payload: (Merchantman) 18,500kg (40,790lb)

V.953 Vanguard PK-MVF is seen departing Heathrow en route to Jakarta in 1975 wearing the original Merpati colours. Altogether, Merpati operated nine different Vanguards and they operated the world's last passenger Vanguard flight in 1987. (Author's collection)

The only 'Vanguard' now capable of running her engines is this ex-British Airways Merchantman at the Brooklands Museum in Surrey. I witnessed the spectacular arrival of G-APEP on the short Weybridge runway on 17th October 1996. (Author)

A whole series of publicity shots were taken of this BOAC/Cunard Super VC-10 G-ASGD. I think this view emphasises the beauty of this type especially the shape of the tailplane. G-ASGD was bought by the Royal Air Force for spares in May 1981. (Brooklands Museum Archives)

VICKERS VC-10 & SUPER VC-10

Vickers Aviation Ltd
Brooklands and Wisley
Aerodromes, Surrey, England

Just as the Trident was produced to meet the specific requirements of BEA, so the VC-10 was also encumbered with a list of specifications that were made by a major British airline, in this case BOAC. Because of their need for a long-range jet airliner which could operate from the hot and high airports at Kano, Nairobi and Johannesburg, BOAC specified a high performance aeroplane that could safely depart these airports with a full load of 15,422kg (34,000lb). The subsequent poor sales of the VC-10 series can be attributed to BOAC's strict requirements and the fact that by the time the VC-10 entered service, most of the airports on BOAC's Empire routes had extended their runways thereby allowing them to accept the less sprightly 707s and DC-8s.

Back in 1955, Vickers suffered a huge disappointment when the British Ministry of Supply cancelled their Type 1000 jet airliner. The prototype, about 80% complete at the time, was chopped up for scrap, but thankfully not all the work on the V.1000 was wasted. Some features were adopted and utilised in the new Vickers Type 1100 VC-10, including the power-operated flying–control surfaces, the variable incidence tailplane and the wing/fuselage frame design.

The prototype VC-10 (unlike previous Vickers commercial airliners it was not given a name) was ceremonially rolled out of its hangar at Brooklands on 15th April 1962.

After two months of resonance tests, systems checks and engine runs, Captain Jock Bryce and co-pilot Brian Trubshaw flew G-ARTA from the short runway at Weybridge to the flight test centre at Wisley on 29th June 1962.

BOAC had initially deposited a letter of intent to buy 35 VC-10s in May 1957, followed by a firm contract in January 1958. After the Super VC-10 had been announced in 1961, BOAC revised its order to 12 VC-10s and 30 'Supers'; however, this was altered once again when they reduced the number of Super VC-10s required to 17. The first paying passengers who could 'try a little VC-10-derness', as the BOAC advert memorably claimed, were on the Heathrow to Lagos service on 29th April 1964.

The Vickers Type 1150 Super VC-10 was developed to fulfil an additional BOAC requirement for a larger passenger load on their North Atlantic routes where the available runway length was not such a problem as it was in Africa and Asia. The main differences in the Super VC-10 were a fuselage stretched by 3.96m (13ft), higher powered (98kN/22,500lb) Conway RCo 43 engines and extra fuel tankage in the fin. The first BOAC Super VC-10 flew on 7th May 1964 and the first service was from London to New York on 1st April 1965.

In 1961, British United Airways' chief Freddie Laker ordered two Type 1103 VC-10s with large forward freight doors for convertible passenger/freight services. Other operators to specify this variant were Ghana Airways, East African Airways and the Royal Air Force. In September 1961, the RAF ordered five VC-10s (later increased to 11). These would be known as the VC-10 C.1 and be used in a variety of roles including troop transport (150 rear-facing seats), medevac (78 stretchers) and freighting.

As the VC-10 and Super VC-10 were withdrawn from airline use, the RAF were able to obtain several examples that had previously been operated by EAA (4 Super VC-10), BA (14 Super VC-10) and Gulf Air (5 VC-10). These aircraft were converted to aerial tankers at Bristol Filton reappearing as K.2s (VC-10) and K.3 (Super). The RAF currently operates the only flying examples of the VC-10/Super VC-10 (24 in total).

Four aircraft are preserved in museums. Brooklands has the ex-BUA/BCAL/Sultan of Oman VC-10, Cosford has an ex-BOAC VC-10, the UAE Government VC-10 is preserved at Hermeskeil in Germany and Duxford has the only preserved Super VC-10.

Specifications (for the VC-10)

Span: 44.55m (142ft 2in)
Length: 48.36m (158ft 8in)
Engines: Four 93.5kN (21,000lb)
    Rolls-Royce Conway RCo 42 Mk.540 turbofans
Cruise speed: 885 km/h (480 kts)
Accommodation: 135

British Airways' VC-10 G-ARVF was leased to the Government of the United Arab Emirates between 1974 and 1981. This aircraft is currently preserved at the incredible Hermeskeil Museum in Germany. (Author's collection)

The world's only preserved Super VC-10 is G-ASGC at Duxford. Acquired by them in 1980, it is displayed in BOAC/Cunard colours and is regularly opened up for visitors to view the cabin. (Author)

This dramatic shot of VS-44A N41881 was taken at Catalina Island. Captained by Wilton R 'Dick' Probert, the President of Avalon Air Transport (Catalina Air Lines), this aircraft flew a Long Beach to Catalina Island service for ten years from 1957. (R Probert, Aero Technology)

VOUGHT SIKORSKY VS-44A

Vought-Sikorsky Aircraft Division
Stratford
Connecticut, USA

Developed from the unique XPBS-1 Navy patrol bomber which first flew in August 1937, the three VS-44As ordered by American Export Airlines in July 1940 for their proposed transatlantic services were the only examples of this flying boat built. The general public had their first chance to see the four-cabin design when a mock-up was displayed at the New York World Fair.

The legendary Captain Charles Blair, the Chief Pilot of American Export Airlines, first flew the VS-44A on 18th January 1942, and the type made its first transatlantic flight in June of that year. American Export gave each of the three aircraft names, 'Excalibur' 'Exeter' and 'Excambian'.

'Excalibur' did not survive for very long. She crashed on take-off at Botwood, Newfoundland in October 1942. However the remaining two VS-44As were flown extensively throughout the war, achieving a total of 405 Atlantic crossings between New York and Foynes, the flying boat terminal on the River Shannon in the west of Ireland. The flying boats, carrying the Navy designation JR2S-1, were crewed by AE civilians but flown under Naval Air Transport Service orders and painted in dull military colours.

After the war, 'Exeter' was employed on gun running missions to Paraguay, but sank in the River Plate whilst on a 'clandestine' supply flight in Uruguay in August 1947. The surviving aircraft, 'Excambian', commenced a

series of trips to Iceland in the late 1940s, but by 1948 she was impounded for non-payment of fees in Baltimore. An imaginative plan to operate her as a flying trading post in South America came to nought and she was eventually withdrawn from use in the harbour at Ancon, north of Lima, Peru.

With a rising demand for passenger services from Long Beach, California to Catalina Island, Dick Probert of Long Beach-based Avalon Air Transport bought the hulk in 1957 and restored her to airworthy condition. Fitted with 47 seats, 'Excambian' flew the 12-minute schedule for 10 years, before being sold to Antilles Air Boats for services in the Virgin Islands. In January 1969, after a couple of years flying in the Caribbean sunshine, a landing accident forced the grounding of the aircraft at St.Thomas. In 1976 this unique aircraft was moved to the Naval Air Museum in Pensacola, Florida, having been donated to them by Antilles Air Boats.

After seven years of virtual neglect, the Naval Air Museum gave the flying boat to the Bradley Air Museum (New England Air Museum since 1984) in Windsor Locks, Connecticut on permanent loan. 'Excambian' was dismantled and transported by barge back to its birthplace in Connecticut in April 1983. Thankfully, the restoration process was sponsored by dozens of local companies with Sikorsky Aircraft being the major player. In October 1998, after a painstaking eleven-

year restoration involving many retired engineers who had worked on the original aircraft, 'Excambian' was towed outside for publicity photographs to be taken. Painted in full American Export Airlines colours, this unique and magnificent flying boat is now protected from the elements and is displayed inside the museum hall.

Specifications

Span: 37.8m (124ft 0in)
Length: 23.21m (76ft 2in)
Engines: Four 895kW (1,200hp)
  P&W R-1830 S1C3G Twin Wasp Radial pistons
Cruise speed: 282km/h (175 mph)
Accommodation: 26 passengers (later 47)
  or 16 in sleeper berths

Another view of N41881 in a revised colour scheme alongside its pier at Long Beach in California. This aircraft was sold to Charles Blair's Antilles Airboats in 1967 who named it 'Mother Goose' because the rest of their fleet were Grumman Goose amphibians. (Aviation Hobby Shop)

The 'Excambian' as she is today. Preserved inside the huge hangar at the New England Air Museum, N41881 sits on her beaching gear and displays the colours of American Export Airlines which it carried in the mid-1940s. (New England Air Museum)

Indispensible companion volumes –

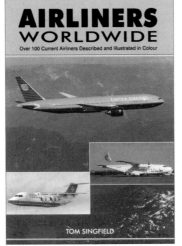

Interest in the airliners of the world continues to grow and with it demands for better reference material. Now, following on from the highly popular full colour format of *Airlines Worldwide,* comes a companion volume, devoted to the wide variety of types that ply the world's airways.

Ranging from the humble 15 seat feederliner to the huge Boeing 747-400, the book provides full colour illustrations of the major types, and roams the planet for rare and colourful examples. Detail given includes development, conversions and sub-series, number built and number in service. Also included is a listing of the airlines using each type.

The author, an air traffic controller, has scoured the world for the illustrations for this book and provided an informative but highly readable reference to each aircraft. From Anglo-French Concorde to DHC Twin Otter, Airbus A340 to Beech 1900D, Douglas Dakota to Boeing 777 – full details of the airliner workhorses of the late 1990s are all there.

An excellent reference, providing at-a-glance information on how widespread a type is, how long it has been in service and operators worldwide.

Softback, 240 x 170 mm, 128 pages. 134 full colour photographs
1 85780 056 7   published August 1997
UK £11.95 / US $19.95

The third edition of this enormously popular reference provides details of the major airlines of the world, including base, call-signs and codes, brief history, route structure and types operated or on order, is in preparation.

The major feature is its superb large size full colour photographs providing vibrant detail of current colour schemes.

This new edition has been completely revised and updated to take into account the fast-changing airline business with new types always coming into service. Several once familiar names have quietly gone out of business whilst there is a never-ending stream of 'start-up' operators.

Softback, 240 x 170 mm, c384 pages. About 360 full colour photographs
1 85780 103 2   Autumn 2000
UK c£18.95 / US c$34.95

AIRLINE TAIL COLOURS
550 colour illustrations to aid in the quick recognition of airlines (2nd edn)

B I Hengi

New edition!
Softback,
150 x 105 mm,
160 pages
c550 col photos
1 85780 104 0
Summer 2000
**UK c£7.95 /
US c$12.95**